P9-DFI-641

The ADHD Workbook for Kids

Helping Children Gain Self-Confidence, Social Skills & Self-Control

LAWRENCE E. SHAPIRO, PH.D.

Instant Help Books
A Division of New Harbinger Publications, Inc.

Publisher's Note

This publication is designed to provide accurate and authoritative information in regard to the subject matter covered. It is sold with the understanding that the publisher is not engaged in rendering psychological, financial, legal, or other professional services. If expert assistance or counseling is needed, the services of a competent professional should be sought.

Distributed in Canada by Raincoast Books

Copyright © 2010 by Lawrence E. Shapiro
       Instant Help Books
       A Division of New Harbinger Publications, Inc.
       5674 Shattuck Avenue
       Oakland, CA 94609
       www.newharbinger.com

Cover design by Amy Shoup

Illustrations by Julie Olsen

All Rights Reserved

Printed in the United States of America

Library of Congress Cataloging-in-Publication Data

Shapiro, Lawrence E.
  The ADHD workbook for kids : helping children gain self-confidence, social skills, and self-control / Lawrence E. Shapiro.
    p. cm.
  ISBN 978-1-57224-766-6
  1. Attention-deficit hyperactivity disorder. I. Title.
  RJ506.H9S527 2010
  618.92'85890076--dc22

                       2010012873

17   16   15

15   14   13   12   11

TABLE OF CONTENTS

Section III: Making and Keeping Friends

Section IV: Feeling Good About Yourself

A Letter to Parents

Being the parent of a child with ADHD requires an extra amount of patience, a special kind of dedication, and a willingness to be an advocate for your child even when no one seems to understand his special needs. (Note: ADHD affects both boys and girls, but boys are about three times more likely than girls to have this problem. Respecting the statistics, I will use masculine pronouns more often than feminine pronouns throughout the book.)

It also requires some very specific knowledge and skills. Let's face it, many things that other parents take for granted, you cannot. You probably worry more about your child's behavior than other parents you know. And well you should. Children with ADHD often say and do things that get them into trouble at home and at school. If you are like most parents of children with ADHD, you also worry about your child's school performance. Many children with ADHD have above-average academic potential, but their problems in organization and in completing work make them perennial underachievers. And while extra school help may be available, it is often not enough.

Most children with ADHD also have problems making and keeping friends, and this is a great concern for parents. It is hard for parents to see their child being ignored when invitations for birthday parties are passed around or siting home alone instead of having a play-date. Some children with ADHD have even more serious social problems. They are teased by classmates, excluded from recess games, and socially isolated.

Then there is the problem of self-esteem. Children with ADHD are often magnets for criticism and negative attention. And if your child is on medication for ADHD, he might have his own concerns about why he is different from other children.

I have written this workbook to help your child learn new emotional, behavioral, and social skills in four major areas of concern: behavior, school success, social development, and self-esteem. Some people call these skills "emotional intelligence." Researchers tell us that emotional-intelligence skills can be taught just like other skills, such as reading, hitting a baseball, or playing a violin. Like these other skills, emotional-intelligence skills need to be taught in a systematic way, and they need to be practiced and reinforced.

That is what this workbook attempts to do, and you can help. Explain the concepts to your child if he seems confused or unaware. When you see your child trying his new skills, make sure to give him plenty of praise.

Please be aware that this workbook has been written as a supplement to a comprehensive treatment program, which should include the use of behavior modification in the home, classroom modifications, and in some cases, specialized tutoring and counseling.

There are no simple answers for children with ADHD, and every child has unique needs. But it is my hope that with your patient guidance, and with good support from your school, your child will achieve the happiness and success that we all wish for our children.

Sincerely,

Lawrence E. Shapiro, Ph.D.

A Letter to Kids

What is it like for you to have ADHD? I have known lots of kids with ADHD, and they tell me it is not really a problem most of the time, but sometimes it can be a pain in the you-know-what.

Kids with ADHD tell me that they get into trouble more often than other kids do. They tell me that their teachers and parents are always saying things like "I know you can do better if you just try a little harder," even when they've tried very hard in the first place! Most kids with ADHD tell me that they don't have many friends and that sometimes their classmates are mean to them.

I've written this workbook to help you with some of these problems, and I hope it will help you. In each activity, you'll learn to handle a different aspect of your ADHD a little better, and you'll also have some fun while you learn. I've included lots of activities that kids enjoy, like drawing and mazes. But I wouldn't be honest if I said that these activities don't require some work, too. And the more you work, the more you will learn, just like in school.

Each activity will teach you a new skill. The activities in Section I will teach you ways to behave that will keep you out of trouble. The activities in Section II will teach you how to do better in school. In Section III, you'll learn some new ways to make friends and have more fun with the friends you already have. And in Section IV, you'll learn some things about yourself and what makes you such a unique and special kid.

Some of activities you will be able to do yourself, and some may require help from your parents or teachers. If you have a counselor, he or she will probably want to help you with these activities, too.

There are lots of people who want to help you be happy, healthy, and successful every day of your life—and I'm one of them!

Best of luck,

Dr. Larry

Section I
Learning Self-Control

Most kids with ADHD have problems with their behavior. It is not that they are "bad" but rather that their behavior doesn't fit with what their parents and teachers expect. Kids with ADHD may not remember the rules and may get in trouble for breaking them. They may have trouble sitting still in class or remembering to raise their hands to be called on. They may talk too loudly at home or even with their friends.

The activities in this section will help you learn new behaviors to get along better with other people, including your parents, your teachers, and even your friends.

For You to Know

Kids with ADHD sometimes forget to think before they act. They may forget about certain rules and what will happen to them if they break these rules. But you can learn to think before you act and to avoid doing the things that make adults angry.

Chris and David were best friends who played together almost every Saturday. David had a castle set up in his basement, with knights and horses and even a fierce dragon. Chris loved to play with the knights, and one Saturday, he wanted to have a jousting tournament. But after a while, David said he was bored and wanted to ride bikes instead.

Chris said, "I can ride my bike anytime. But I never get to play with a castle like this at my house, and it's so cool."

"Well, I play with the castle all the time, and I'm bored," David replied, "and since you're at my house, I get to make the rules about what we do."

Chris knew David did get to make the rules about his toys in his house. But he wasn't very happy about going outside, and he thought that David was being too bossy. When David turned to go upstairs, Chris put one of the knights into his pocket. It was a black knight waving a sword over his head.

Later that day, Chris's mom saw him playing with the black knight. "Where did you get that?" she asked. "It doesn't look familiar."

"I found it," Chris said, not able to think of a better answer.

"Where did you find it?" his mom asked, moving closer to him and looking at him suspiciously.

"I don't remember," Chris said. "It was just in my pocket."

"Well, maybe we need to have a talk about how toys just get into your pocket," said Chris's mom. From the look in her eye, Chris knew that this was not going to be a talk he would enjoy.

Helping Children Gain Self-Confidence, Social Skills, and Self-Control

Have you ever taken anything that didn't belong to you? What happened?

_____

_____

_____

_____

For You to Do

Think about the things you have done in the past that got you into trouble. Maybe you did something that you knew was wrong and you are sorry that you did it. Or maybe you did something that got you into trouble, but you didn't really think it was wrong. If you think before you act, you can avoid doing these things. You won't have to feel bad, and you won't get punished.

This Six-Point Decision Scale can help you decide whether what you want to do is a good idea or a bad one. To use the scale, just assign a number to the thing you want to do. Here is what the numbers mean:

1 = This decision will help people.

2 = This decision won't hurt anyone, and it will make me happy.

3 = This decision will make me happy, but it really isn't good for me.

4 = This decision will make me happy, but it may make other people mad.

5 = This decision is against the rules.

6 = This decision is against the law.

In the chart below, write down five things you did in the past that got you into trouble. Then use the Six-Point Decision Scale to rate each of these things.

Things That Got Me into Trouble	Decision Scale Rating (1 to 6)

... *And More to Do*

Once you learn the Six-Point Decision Scale, it will help you decide whether a behavior is a good idea or a bad one. You *can* do things that are a number 1 or 2, but you should *not* do things that are a 3, 4, or 5. Here are some situations you can use to practice. Put the decision rating next to each behavior. Then ask an adult to check your answers.

_____ Susie wouldn't let Shauna play with her group at recess.

_____ Ethan snuck out of bed after his parents were asleep, and he ate six cookies.

_____ Tyrone wanted to ride his bike, but he decided to make a get-well card for his grandma first.

_____ Karen made a thank-you card for her aunt Emma.

_____ Abby kept interrupting her father while he was on the phone.

_____ Tanya spent two hours playing video games instead of doing her homework.

_____ Elizabeth was mad at Isabelle, so she sent her a mean e-mail, pretending that she was Isabelle's friend Mark.

You Can Predict What Other People Will Do

For You to Know

Many kids with ADHD don't predict the consequences of their actions. Even though you probably know what will happen if you break a rule, you may do it anyway. But you can predict what might happen in most situations if you really think about it. When you learn to predict what other people will do and what might happen to you, you will find it easier to control your behavior.

Every Monday, Marybeth's teacher gave out a list of new spelling words. Every Thursday, the class had a spelling test.

On Monday night, Marybeth was supposed to start learning the words, but she watched her favorite television show instead. On Tuesday, Marybeth was supposed to spend fifteen minutes learning the spelling words again, but she had soccer practice. Then she ate dinner, did some math homework, and later went to bed. She didn't spend any time on her spelling.

On Wednesday, Marybeth was supposed to practice her spelling words with one of her parents. But her mom was busy taking care of her little brother and her dad had a headache, so Marybeth didn't ask either of them to help her. On Thursday, Marybeth took her spelling test. On Friday, she got back her test, marked with an F. Fifteen of the twenty words were spelled wrong.

All the tests had to be signed by a parent and turned in the next Monday. After school, Marybeth gave her spelling test to her mom to sign. "What happened?" Marybeth's mom asked. "How did you get such a bad grade on this test? You are a pretty good speller."

"I don't know," Marybeth said. "I don't know what happened."

But you know, don't you?

Have you ever gotten a bad grade because you didn't study? Tell what happened.

_____

_____

_____

_____

For You to Do

Can you predict what will happen to the kids on the left? Draw a line from each picture on the left to the picture on the right that shows what will probably happen.

Helping Children Gain Self-Confidence, Social Skills, and Self-Control

... And More to Do

When you stop to think about it, you can probably predict the ways that grown-ups will react to different things that you do. Here's your chance to practice:

Write down three things you might do that will get you a hug.

1. _____

2. _____

3. _____

Write down three things you might do that will get you yelled at or punished.

1. _____

2. _____

3. _____

Write down three things you might do that will get you good grades.

1. _____

2. _____

3. _____

Write down three things you might do that will make someone say "Thank you."

1. _____

2. _____

3. _____

For You to Know

Being easily distracted is one of the things that almost all kids with ADHD share. They usually get bored more easily than kids without ADHD. They are often very smart, but still get bad grades. It might be because they don't complete their classroom assignments, their homework, or even their tests. But you can learn to stay interested in something even if it seems hard or boring at first. A kid with ADHD who is interested in something can work for hours.

Kyle's parents went to school for a teacher's conference. Kyle's teacher, Mrs. Macey, said, "Kyle is a very bright boy, and I really like having him in the class. But he never finishes an assignment unless I stand over him. I've thought about bringing his desk right next to mine and keeping an eye on him while he works, but that wouldn't be fair to the rest of the kids who need my attention."

Kyle's mom said, "Kyle is the same way around the house. He'll start to clean up his room, and as long as I'm right there, he is fine. But if I have to go away for even five minutes, he starts to do something else. I don't know why Kyle can't seem to finish anything."

When Kyle's parents got home that night, they asked the babysitter, Jamie, what Kyle had been doing. "Kyle has been doing the same thing for three hours," Jamie said. "I showed him how to make origami swans, and look, he's made nearly a hundred!"

Kyle's mom and dad looked at each other, wondering what made their son work hard on some things and not others.

You Can Keep Trying
Even When You Are Bored

What activities keep you interested? What activities do you find boring? What do you usually do when you are bored?

_____

_____

_____

_____

For You to Do

Write down five things you love to do that never make you bored.

1. _____

2. _____

3. _____

4. _____

5. _____

Now write down five things you have to do but find really boring.

1. _____

2. _____

3. _____

4. _____

5. _____

Next to each of the things you find boring, write down what would make it less boring. For example, you might not like making your bed, but if you play music while you do it, it won't be so bad. Or you might not like doing homework, but you might like it better if a parent works in the same room and keeps you company. Be creative and see if you can think of some good ways to make things you have to do less boring.

... And More to Do

If you are like Kyle, you will work hard on something that interests you, but not on something that is boring. Sometimes you can make things more interesting. For example, Amelia didn't like raking leaves but when her father said, "I'll give you a nickel for every five minutes that you rake," Amelia thought that would be fun. She raked for ten minutes, and her father gave her two nickels. She raked for twenty minutes more, and her father said, "Now you've earned four more nickels." When Amelia had raked leaves for seventy minutes more, her dad gave her fourteen nickels. Now she had one dollar.

Ask your parents if you can earn a nickel for every five minutes you do a special chore. What will it be? Washing the car? Cleaning out a closet? If it takes a long time, that's good, not bad. The longer you work, the more money you will earn!

If your parents say it is okay, ask them to put out twenty nickels next to a small jar where you are going to do your chore. Do you have a watch you can use to time how long you work? If not, ask your parent or another adult to keep track of the time. Put a nickel in the jar after every five minutes you work. But be fair! If you don't work for five minutes, you don't get a nickel. See if you can earn a whole dollar, like Amelia did, or maybe even more!

For You to Know

Kids with ADHD have a hard time waiting for something they want. They would rather have a small cookie right now than a much larger cookie in two hours. But you can learn to be more patient and enjoy the larger cookie later! Learning to be more patient will make it easier for you to get along with other people.

Heather couldn't wait for her mom to serve dinner. It was meatballs and spaghetti, Heather's favorite! But her mom was on the phone, and Heather could see that dinner wasn't ready.

"When are we eating?" Heather asked. She knew she wasn't supposed to interrupt her mom on the phone, but sometimes her mom didn't seem to mind.

Heather's mom held up five fingers. Then she repeated the gesture three times more.

"Twenty minutes?" Heather asked. Her mom nodded.

Twenty minutes later, Heather went back into the kitchen, ready to eat. Her mom was still on the phone, the meatballs were still simmering, and the unopened box of spaghetti still sat on the counter.

"Where's dinner?" Heather asked loudly. "You said it would be twenty minutes."

Her mom held up one finger to her lips, then pointed to the phone, indicating that Heather should stop asking questions and be quiet.

"But I'm hungry!" Heather said. "You can talk after dinner."

Her mom shook her head back and forth. Heather knew that her mom was getting angry, but Heather was angry, too. "I'm starving," she shouted. "I need my dinner!"

Heather's mom looked at her daughter with a cold stare that Heather didn't like at all. Then she put down the phone and said, "You won't collapse if dinner is a little late. Now go to your room, and don't come down until I get you. And if you interrupt me just one more time, you won't be getting any dinner tonight."

Heather stomped off to her room, thinking, "I have the meanest mom in the whole world."

Did you ever get into trouble for being impatient? What happened?

_____

_____

_____

_____

For You to Do

Have you ever had someone ask you, "Can't you just sit still and be patient?" Most kids with ADHD hear this all too often, but they are not the only ones who have difficulty waiting. Even adults can have a hard time being patient. Maybe you've been in a traffic jam where people are honking at each other and even yelling out the window. Or maybe you've seen an adult get angry at a computer that was running slowly.

Most people don't like to wait for things, but some things can't be rushed. Here are five things that can't be rushed. Can you think of five more?

- Growing up

- Your birthday

- A visit to the doctor's office

- Learning to play a sport or an instrument

- A garden

1. _____

2. _____

3. _____

4. _____

5. _____

A "Patience Box" can help when you have to be patient. Ask a parent for a shoe box, and decorate it if you like. On small pieces of paper, write down all the things you can think of to do when you have to be patient. For example, you might write, "E-mail a friend" or "Make a sculpture out of clay." You can ask your parents or even your friends to write down some interesting activities, too. The next time you have a hard time waiting, close your eyes and reach into your Patience Box. Pick up to three activities to do, and then select the one that you think would be most fun.

Helping Children Gain Self-Confidence, Social Skills, and Self-Control

... And More to Do

Very few kids find it easy to be patient, but it is important to learn to be patient even when you don't feel like it. Here is an activity that requires patience. See if you can do it without getting angry or upset. The more patience you have, the easier it will be.

The Patience Maze

This maze doesn't look too hard, does it? Can you do it without crossing a single line *and using the hand opposite the one you write with*? In other words, if you are right-handed, use your left hand; if you are left-handed, use your right hand. Use a pencil and go slowly. If you cross the line even once, erase what you have done and start over.

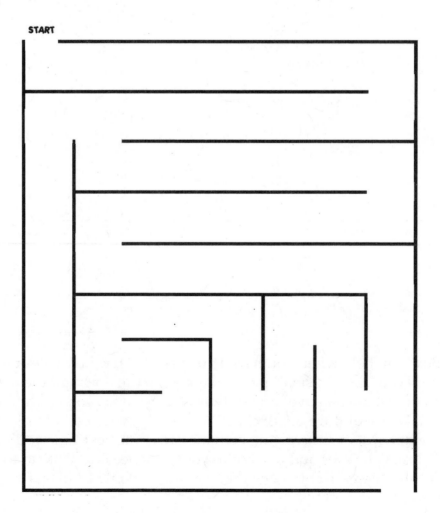

You Can Learn to Be a Good Listener

For You to Know

Many kids with ADHD say things out loud as soon as they think of them, but other people find this very annoying. Whether you are in class or just talking to a friend, it is important to know when to talk and when to listen. Being a good listener is not as easy as it sounds. You have to wait your turn to speak, and then you have to know when to stop speaking. You also have to know when it is important to not speak at all.

"Catherine, can you tell me what the biggest animal on earth is?" Mrs. Petropolis asked.

"A dinosaur?" Catherine said.

"That's stupid," Josh said. "There aren't any dinosaurs on earth anymore."

"Josh, I didn't call on you," Mrs. Petropolis said, "and calling someone stupid is against our rules. You know better."

"Sorry," Josh said, "but dinosaurs haven't been around for millions of years."

"How about you, Brooke?" Mrs. Petropolis said. "Can you tell me what animal is the biggest in the world?"

"An elephant?" Brooke said.

"Nope," Josh said, "it's a whale, a blue whale. Right, Mrs. Petropolis?"

Mrs. Petropolis walked over to Josh's desk and leaned down so she could look at him eye to eye. "You are right, Josh, and you are right a lot of the time, but that's not the point. Your answer is right, but your behavior is wrong, and I have to take points away from your chart. I've told you over and over not to answer unless you raise your hand and are called on. I don't want to hear you speak again today unless you are called on."

Josh's feelings were hurt. He thought, "I can't help it if I'm the only one who knows the answers in the whole school. It's not my fault."

Helping Children Gain Self-Confidence, Social Skills, and Self-Control

Have you ever gotten into trouble for speaking without being called on in class? What happened?

_____

_____

_____

_____

For You to Do

Scientists tell us that the words we use are not as important in having a conversation as our body language. Body language consists of our gestures (how we use our hands), our posture (how we hold our bodies), our facial expressions, and, in particular, our eye contact (whether or not we look at the person we are listening or speaking to).

Look at the pictures below and put a check on the ones that show kids who know how to be good listeners. Put an X on the pictures of the kids who don't look like good listeners. Write down the things that tell you whether or not they are good listeners.

_____

_____

_____

_____

_____

_____

_____

_____

_____

_____

_____

_____

... And More to Do

It's easy to see how calling out at school can get you into trouble, but the rules are not always so clear outside of school. You don't have to raise your hand to talk to your parents or friends, but you do have to speak and listen, back and forth, and back and forth again. It is a little like going on a seesaw—you have to take turns, or it just won't work. Here are some rules to follow:

- Don't interrupt someone who is talking.

- Listen to what the other person just said. What you say next should be related to that.

- Don't try to show off how much you know.

- Try not to talk too fast or too loudly.

- Ask questions about what the other person is thinking, and wait for the answers.

- Watch how people react to what you are saying. (Their body language may say more than their words.)

Here are some situations you might find yourself in. Circle the ones when you shouldn't speak at all, unless you are asked a question.

Taking a test	At religious services
At dinner	Visiting someone in the hospital
In the library	When a baby is sleeping nearby
At a basketball game	During a checkup at the doctor's office
Crossing the street	In an arcade

For You to Know

Most kids with ADHD have a hard time sitting still without fidgeting. People sometimes say that a child who has a hard time sitting still is hyperactive, or hyper. "Hyper" just means "a lot of something" or "more than usual." So if you are hyperactive, you are just more active than most kids. Wanting to move around doesn't make you a bad kid—not at all—but it may annoy your parents or your teachers or even other kids.

"Can't you stop fidgeting," Mrs. Rose asked Justin. "You shouldn't be tapping your feet when Annie is giving her book report."

"I'm sorry," Justin said, and he pressed his feet hard against the floor.

A few minutes later, Mrs. Rose spoke to Justin again. "Now you're moving your head back and forth, like you're listening to music. Are you listening to music?"

"No," said Justin, and then he thought about the question. "Well, I was thinking about a song I heard this morning."

"Well, it's very distracting for the rest of us when you keep moving around," said Mrs. Rose. "Think about what is going on and try to be still."

"Okay," said Justin. "I'll keep still."

But after a few more minutes, Justin felt like twiddling his thumbs. He knew it would annoy Mrs. Rose, but he really felt like doing it! He sat on his hands, but all he could think about was how much he wanted to twiddle his thumbs. He didn't hear a word of Annie's book report. He couldn't wait to go out to recess, and that was a whole hour away.

Do you ever feel like you can't sit still? Write down what you do when that happens.

_____

_____

_____

_____

For You to Do

Sometimes kids take medication to help them sit still and stop their fidgeting, but medication is not the only answer. Learning to control your body is something everyone can do, and an exercise called isometrics may help (and may even make you stronger). In isometrics, you don't really move. You just press your arms or legs against each other or against another object. Try these isometric exercises:

- Clasp your hands together in front of you and push them against each other. Push as hard as you can for one minute, then relax.

- Push your knees together as hard as you can for one minute, then relax.

- Place your hands on the table and push the table down into the floor. Do this for one minute, then relax.

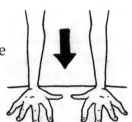

- Press your feet on the floor for one minute, then relax.

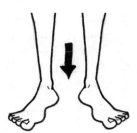

Helping Children Gain Self-Confidence, Social Skills, and Self-Control

Activity 6 You Can Learn to Sit Still

As you can see, doing isometric exercises involves putting pressure on your muscles without actually moving them. They can be done almost anywhere, at any time. When kids with ADHD are feeling fidgety or having a hard time paying attention, they find that these exercises are particularly helpful.

Can you think of three more isometric exercises? Remember that this kind of exercise involves pushing or pulling a group of muscles, but not actually moving. Write down your ideas here:

1. _____

2. _____

3. _____

... And More to Do

There are other things that can help you feel calmer and control your body when you feel like fidgeting. Some kids with ADHD wear special weighted clothes or have weighted stuffed animals to put on their laps.

Some kids take short exercise breaks every ten or fifteen minutes; they stand up and stretch their muscles. You can take these breaks yourself when you are at home, but if you are in class, your teacher must say it's okay. Some kids have little toys that keep their hands busy, like a ball to squeeze. Adults often don't mind when kids use these toys, because it helps kids concentrate.

Activity 7   You Can Learn to Follow Instructions

For You to Know

Kids with ADHD pay attention to lots of things at the same time. Grown-ups say that they are distractible. When you are distractible, it is hard to pay attention to one thing at a time, and that can make it hard for you to follow instructions. You may need to have instructions written down or have instructions broken down into smaller steps.

Bailey was working on her math problems when her teacher came over with a scowl on her face.

"What did I ask you to do?" asked Mrs. Fried.

"You said to work on our math problems," Bailey replied. She definitely knew that this was what Mrs. Fried had said.

Mrs. Fried didn't look happy with Bailey's explanation. She said, "I told you to work on your math problems, then hand them in, and then take out your silent-reading books. Look around you. Everyone is reading their books, except you."

"Oh," said Bailey, "I guess I didn't hear the last part of it."

Mrs. Fried said, "Well, Bailey, maybe you'd better listen more carefully."

Do adults ever get mad at you for not listening? Write down what happens.

_____

_____

_____

_____

For You to Do

Kids with ADHD usually don't have problems hearing, but they may have problems remembering what they are told because they aren't paying attention. There are many tricks you can learn to help you be better at following instructions.

Look at the sentences below. See if you can unscramble the key words in each sentence to learn the tricks that can help you be a better listener. If you need help, the answers are upside down at the bottom of the page.

1. Look at the *noeprs* who is talking to you.

2. *eaRept* what you are told.

3. Ask that directions be *tnewrit* down. As you complete each step, *khcec* it off.

4. Use an audio *ordrecer* in class to record your assignments.

5. Carry a *botokeno* to write down your assignments.

5. Carry a *notebook* to write down your assignments.

4. Use an audio *recorder* in class to record your assignments.

3. Ask that directions be *written* down. As you complete each step, *check* it off.

2. *Repeat* what you are told.

1. Look at the *person* who is talking to you.

... And More to Do

Some things may distract you more than others. Read this list of things that often distract kids with ADHD; you can use the blank lines to add other distractions. On a scale of 1 to 5, rate how often each distracts you, where 1 = never and 5 = always. When you are done, ask one of your parents to rate these things as well. Do you agree about the things that distract you? Finally, go back and see if you can think of ways to deal with the distractions you rated 3, 4, or 5. Your parents or teachers may have some suggestions.

Things That Distract Me	My Rating (1 to 5)	My Parent's Rating (1 to 5)	Ways to Deal with This Distraction
People talking			
People moving around			
Noise of any kind			
Things on my desk			
Getting an idea			
Music			

For You to Know

Adults expect kids to follow lots of rules. There are rules about how to treat other kids, about how to act at the table, about how to be safe on a bike, and about staying on schedule in class. There are rules everywhere! Some rules are written down, but most are not, or they may not be clear. That can make it hard for kids with ADHD to remember all of these rules. Depending on the rule you break, you will almost always get into trouble.

Caryn didn't like schedules. When her dad said it was time to go to bed, Caryn would always want to stay up longer. When her mom said it was time to go to school, Caryn wanted to stay in bed. She was supposed to do her homework right after dinner, but she would usually find some reason why she couldn't do it just then. Sometimes she wouldn't even start her homework until it was almost her bedtime.

At school, Caryn liked to do things on her own schedule, too, not when the teacher wanted them done. Every morning, her class would have circle time at 9:00, reading at 10:00, and snack at 10:30. But Caryn often wanted her snack at 9:00, and she didn't want to do reading until the afternoon!

Most of the time, Caryn would go along with what her teacher wanted, but sometimes she just didn't feel like it. She would sit and stare out the window, which made her teacher angry.

When her teacher would warn her, "You're going to have to stay in and work during recess," Caryn didn't argue with her teacher; she wouldn't say anything at all.

Do you ever have trouble staying on a schedule or following another rule? Write about it here:

_____

_____

_____

_____

For You to Do

Thinking and talking about rules is probably the best way to remember them. On the chart that follows, five rules have been written in for you, and you have to write in the consequences of breaking these rules. Then write down another five rules that are important to you and the consequences of breaking those rules.

Rule	Consequences of Breaking This Rule
Don't take anything that doesn't belong to you.	
Chew with your mouth closed.	
Wash your hands before you eat.	
Hand in your homework on time.	
Don't use curse words.	

... And More to Do

Your parents and teachers may have different ideas of what rules they think are important for you to remember. Make copies of this blank chart and give one to your parents and another to your teacher. Ask them to write down the five most important rules for you to remember as well as what will happen (the consequences) if you break those rules.

Rule	Consequences of Breaking This Rule
1.	
2.	
3.	
4.	
5.	

Talk to your parents and teachers about why these rules are important. They will appreciate the fact that you are trying to control your behavior, and they will want to help you learn to follow the rules and not get into trouble.

For You to Know

Kids with ADHD often get into trouble. Teachers can get mad at kids who don't sit still. Parents can get mad at kids who don't do their chores or complete their homework. But even if you get into trouble, adults will be more understanding if you are a child who does nice things for others.

Brian was a super nice kid. Everyone said so. He was polite and very considerate. He always said please and thank you. He helped clear the dinner dishes after every meal, and at school he would pick up trash from the hallway or the playground and throw it away. Brian knew that nobody at his school wanted to see lots of litter.

Brian was also a kid with ADHD. He had problems completing his assignments, and his parents and teacher thought that he talked too much. Sometimes Brian would get mad at someone and wouldn't say what was bothering him. His father would say, "It doesn't help when you just sulk around." But Brian had a hard time talking about what was bothering him.

Still, everyone was patient with Brian because he was so nice.

What do you do that is helpful to others? Write it here:

_____

_____

_____

_____

For You to Do

Doing something kind every day is a great way to make your parents and teachers proud of you. It's not hard at all to do something kind every day if you become a "kindness detective." Look for ways to help others throughout the day. You can hold the door for someone, do an extra chore without being asked, or ask if a parent or teacher needs help.

Write down five ways that you can be kind and helpful at home and school. See if you can do a kind act each day. For five days, when you do a kind act, color in a kindness trophy.

1. _____

2. _____

3. _____

4. _____

5. _____

... And More to Do

Lots of people think that being kind is important for everyone. There is even an organization (like a club) for people who try to help others be more kind. You can go to the website www.helpothers.org to get dozens of ideas of ways to be kind and helpful, and you'll also find stories about how people appreciate the kindness of others.

Here are some ideas from this website on how to be kind:

- Give someone a flower.

- Don't wait until February 14 to make valentines; make one today for someone you care about.

- Do something unexpected for your parents, like offering to clean the garage.

- Donate one of your stuffed animals to a hospital.

- Write a thank-you card for a community worker, like a policeman or fireman.

- Sell lemonade and cookies and give the money to a charity.

- Write a note of appreciation to your teacher.

Activity 10   You Can Solve Any Problem

For You to Know

Solving your own problems is part of growing up and taking responsibility for yourself. The more you learn to solve your own problems, the better you will feel about yourself, and your parents and teachers will also appreciate that you are becoming more self-reliant. Learning to solve your own problems doesn't mean that you can't ask for help. If you get stuck trying to solve a problem, it is fine for you to ask someone you trust to help you out.

David copied the math problems his teacher had written on the board, but he didn't understand what to do.

His teacher said, "I want you to take these five problems home and come back tomorrow with the correct answers. Any questions?"

David thought that he probably should ask a question like, "How in the world do you do these problems?" But he thought that everyone else in his class probably knew what to do, and he didn't want to look stupid.

At home, he asked his mom if she knew how to solve the problems. She looked at them for a while, then said, "I have no idea how to do these. I wasn't too good in math. Can you call one of your friends to help out?"

But David didn't have any friends to call. So he just stared at the problems for a few minutes and then stuffed his homework into his backpack. He didn't know what to do, but maybe he would think of something by tomorrow.

What would you have done if you were David?

_____

_____

_____

_____

For You to Do

Everyone has problems to solve. Most of these problems aren't too hard if you just think about them, like what to buy your mother for her birthday or what to wear when the weather is changing. Sometimes kids have big problems to solve along with the smaller ones. What do you do if you are being bullied? What do you do if you don't like your teacher? What do you do if a parent is always mad at you?

The best approach is to think of as many solutions as you can and write them down. This is sometimes called brainstorming. Then go through all of your ideas, see which one is best, and try it. If your first idea doesn't work, you can go back to your list and find another one to try.

See if you can think of at least four possible solutions to these girls' problems. Write them down on the blank lines. Then circle the solution that you think would be the best one.

... And More to Do

Think about some of the big problems you have to solve. Then use this worksheet to write down one of your problems and four possible solutions. Circle the solution you think would be best. After you have tried it, write in what happened. If it didn't work, tell what else you will try.

My Problem _____

Solution 1 _____

Solution 2 _____

Solution 3 _____

Solution 4 _____

What happened after you tried the solution? _____

_____

What else will you try? _____

_____

Activity 11

You Can Be Your Own Coach

For You to Know

Lots of people have learned to talk to themselves in a special way when they are having a hard time. When you talk to yourself that way, you can act like a coach and encourage yourself to try harder.

Lindsay's mom wanted to get her a bike for her birthday, but Lindsay had never learned to ride. "I can't do it," she told her mom. "I tried when I was little, and I just fell off and hurt my knee. Don't you remember?"

"That was years ago," her mom said, "and you're much better coordinated now. Why don't you give it a try?"

Lindsay wanted to ride a bike like all of her friends did. But she was afraid that she would fall off again, and even worse, that her friends would make fun of her if she fell. "I want to learn," she told her mom, "but I'm afraid to fall and look stupid."

"It's okay to be afraid," Lindsay's mom said, "but being afraid doesn't mean that you can't try something that's new or hard. You have to learn to talk back to your fears."

"What do I say?" Lindsay asked. Lindsay wasn't sure how she could talk to a feeling, but she thought her mom must know what she was talking about.

"Well, you just talk to yourself," said her mom. "Say something like, 'I can do this. It's not so hard. I can do lots of things that are harder than riding a bike. It might take me a few tries, but if the other kids can ride a bike, then I can too. And I don't care what I look like. Everybody looks a little silly when they try something new.'"

Is there anything that you have been afraid to try? What could you say to encourage yourself to try it?

_____

_____

_____

_____

You Can Be Your Own Coach

For You to Do

Lots of people say positive things to themselves to control their moods.

Baseball players talk to themselves to help them concentrate and hit the ball. Write down what you think they might say.

_____

_____

Famous rock stars talk to themselves when they are nervous about giving a performance. (Yes, even famous people get nervous. Sometimes they get so nervous that they throw up!) Write down what famous rock stars might say to themselves.

_____

_____

Kids with ADHD sometimes talk to themselves to help them focus on their work. Write down what you could say to yourself to help you keep focused on your schoolwork.

_____

_____

... And More to Do

Now try to do something that has been hard for you, giving yourself a positive pep talk as you try. Write down some things you could say to yourself:

_____

_____

_____

_____

_____

It's easy to be your own coach. Just write down some positive things you could say to yourself, and practice saying them out loud. Next, practice whispering them quietly. Then practice just thinking them.

Activity 12

You Can Keep Your Room Neat

For You to Know

Parents don't like it when their kid's room is a mess. Some parents clean the room themselves and then get mad at their kid for being irresponsible. Some parents punish their kid, and others say, "If you can't keep your room clean, then you can just live in this pigpen." You can avoid fighting with your parents if you just keep your room neat and pick up after yourself each day.

Daniel's family was going to a wedding. "Hurry up," his mom said, "and don't forget to wear your good black shoes."

Daniel put on his new pants, his new white shirt, his belt, and his clip-on tie. He found his dark socks right away. He had a drawer full of socks. But where were his shoes? It had been a long time since Daniel saw his black dress shoes—probably since the school holiday concert, and that was over four months ago!

Daniel looked on the floor of his closet, where he found toys and books along with sneakers and boots and some of his old action figures—but no black shoes. He looked under the bed, where he would throw dirty clothes and toys and even old plates of food when his mom told him to clean his room. It was pretty scary under there, and when he looked for his shoes, he didn't see them.

"We're ready to go," Daniel's father shouted from the hallway. "I'm going to start the car, and you need to get right down here."

Daniel was starting to panic. His mother was going to be mad at him if he didn't have his black shoes, and his father was going to be mad at him if he was late.

The ADHD Workbook for Kids

Have you ever had a problem like Daniel's when your room was a mess? Write about it here:

_____

_____

_____

_____

For You to Do

It's important for you to keep your room straight and clean. It will make your parents happy, and it will be easier for you to find what you want. And you might even find that you like living in a neat room! You can keep your room neat by

- making your bed;

- hanging up your clean clothes or putting them in a drawer;

- putting dirty clothes in the hamper;

- putting away toys and books when you are done with them.

Look carefully at the room below. Put an X on all the things that are wrong with it.

The ADHD Workbook for Kids

... And More to Do

It's not easy to form a new habit, but it helps if you get a reward for trying very hard. Use the chart below to see if you can keep your room neat every day for a whole month. Put a star in the box for every day that your room is neat. Try to get at least fifteen stars; maybe you can get even more! Ask your parents if you can have a special treat or privilege if you get more than fifteen stars.

My Clean Room Chart						
Monday	Tuesday	Wednesday	Thursday	Friday	Saturday	Sunday

Section II
Overcoming School Problems

Lots of kids have problems in school, but kids with ADHD usually have more problems than other kids. Having ADHD means having a hard time paying attention and concentrating on your work, but that is exactly what teachers expect you to do.

School can present other challenges for kids with ADHD as well. To succeed at school, you have to do things on time; you have to keep your work neat and organized; and you have to be aware of all the school rules and respect them. If you have a problem with any of these school challenges, the activities in this section will help. And remember, there are people in your school who can help you as well. Teachers, counselors, school psychologists, tutors, and even school administrators can all help you at school. Don't be afraid to ask for help when you need it!

For You to Know

The United States Congress has passed a special law about kids with ADHD, which shows that the people in charge of the country understand it is hard to be in school when you have ADHD. This law says that schools must have a plan that includes changes (or accommodations) in the regular classroom to help kids with ADHD learn. Some of these accommodations include special places to study, timers to help kids stay focused, untimed tests, and laptop computers and audio recorders for kids who have trouble writing.

Christopher had never really liked school. When he was young, he had speech problems and people at school had a hard time understanding him. Everyone would always ask, "What did you say?" or "Could you say that again?" and he didn't like repeating things over and over.

He also had a hard time sitting still and working at his seat. While the other kids would do math problems or read silently for a half hour or more, Christopher got antsy after ten minutes. He would squirm or look around or talk to his neighbor—and then get into trouble.

Once his teachers found out that Christopher had ADHD, everything changed. His teacher met with Christopher's parents and the school psychologist. His mom and dad said that the meeting was about ways that his teacher could help Christopher do better in school. They made a plan and agreed to meet again in two months to see how that plan was working out.

Some kids don't like to have special classroom accommodations because it makes them feel different from other kids. Other kids think that it is cool to be special. What do you think?

_____

_____

_____

_____

For You to Do

It is up to your teachers to find ways to help you do well in school, and they can get help from the school psychologist or other school staff members. But it will help them if they understand what things are hard for you. Look at the list of problems that kids with ADHD often have, and check off the ones that you have:

☐ I have a hard time understanding what I'm supposed to do.

☐ I have hard time getting things done on time.

☐ I get bored really easily, particularly when I'm doing _____.
                                                      (fill in the blank)

☐ I make a lot of mistakes, and I don't like doing things over.

☐ I have a hard time taking tests.

☐ I have a hard time remembering what to do next.

☐ I never know what my teacher wants me to do.

☐ I have a hard time understanding directions that are written out.

☐ My teacher says that my work is messy.

☐ I can't find things when I want them.

☐ My teacher says that my handwriting is hard to read.

☐ My teacher says I talk too much.

☐ I have a hard time sitting still for long periods of time.

☐ I have a hard time working with other kids.

☐ I have a hard time getting along with my teacher and also with _____.
                                                            (fill in a name)

☐ I often lose things.

☐ I get into trouble at school when I'm outside my classroom.

☐ I don't like recess because _____.
                                        (fill in the reason)

The most important thing to remember is to tell people when you are having a hard time. Show this checklist to your parents and your teacher. Talk to them about what you find hard in school so they can try to make things easier for you.

... And More to Do

There are lots of ways to help kids with ADHD, and maybe you have some of your own ideas. Look at the boy in the picture below. He has ADHD and he doesn't like school at all. Draw in anything that might make him like school better.

Activity 14   You Can Get Ready for School Without a Fuss

For You to Know

Lots of kids have problems getting ready for school on time. Most kids don't like to get out of bed and then rush to get ready for school. Most parents don't like to nag their kids about getting ready on time, and they certainly don't like it when kids are late. And when mornings start off with an argument, the whole day can be ruined. There are some simple things you can do to help you get ready on time in the morning.

On weekends, Alec would sleep late and his parents never minded. But things were very different on school mornings. Alec's alarm would ring and ring, and his father would call, "Get out of bed! You have exactly one hour to get ready!"

Alec would say, "Just a few more minutes," and then he'd fall back asleep.

His mother would come in soon after and wake him up again. One morning, she even pulled him out of bed! That got Alec up, but he was mad at his mom all day.

Even when Alec was out of bed, he moved like he was still asleep. He was slow to shower and slow to dress, and he often wouldn't get down to breakfast until five minutes before his school bus came. Every morning there was lots of nagging and shouting and bad feelings. Alec hated these mornings and so did his parents.

What are you like in the morning? Write down a few sentences that describe your typical morning.

_____

_____

_____

_____

You Can Get Ready for
School Without a Fuss

For You to Do

Being prepared and getting into a positive morning routine is the best way to avoid morning hassles. You can use this checklist to help you remember all the things you have to do the night before and when you wake up. Make fifteen copies of this form and use it every school day for three weeks. Then see if getting ready for school without a fuss has become a habit. Some of the tasks are filled out for you, but you may want to add more. Put the times that you should do each task, and then check it off when it is done.

Day _____   Date _____

Time to Do Each Task	What to Do Before You Go to Bed	Check When Done
	Put your clothes out.	
	Put your homework and school supplies in your backpack.	
	Talk to your parents about what you will have for lunch the next day and whether you will buy it or make it.	
	Set the alarm clock.	

Helping Children Gain Self-Confidence, Social Skills, and Self-Control

Time to Do Each Task	What to Do When You Get Up	Check When Done
	Brush your teeth and wash up.	
	Get dressed.	
	Eat breakfast.	
	Prepare your lunch or get lunch money.	

... And More to Do

There are good habits, and there are bad habits. The girl below is thinking about both her good and bad habits. In the circle below, draw in good habits that kids need to have. In the squares below, draw in bad habits that kids should avoid.

Activity 15   You Can Learn to Be on Time

For You to Know

Most kids with ADHD can tell time without any trouble, but many still have problems being on time, even if they wear wristwatches. Kids with ADHD often say that they get interested in doing something else, and that is why they are late. But if you work at it, you can learn to be on time.

Jon was always late. He missed the bus at least once a week. This made his mother really mad, because she would have to take him to school and then be late for work. He was late for Little League practice so often that his coach wouldn't let him play.

One time, Jon was late returning to class after lunch, so his teacher made him stay after school to clean up the classroom, and his dad had to pick him up. His dad wasn't too happy about that.

Jon got a new watch for his birthday, and his mom said, "Now you don't have to be late at all. Just look at your watch and see what time it is, then make sure you are at the right place at the right time."

Is being on time a problem you have? Write down something that helps you remember to be on time.

_____

_____

_____

_____

For You to Do

Ashley had to clean up her room and do her reading before she could play. She had to be home for dinner and at the table by six o'clock. But Ashley had lots of distractions that kept her from getting things done and from being on time. Can you help Ashley find her way past the things that might distract her?

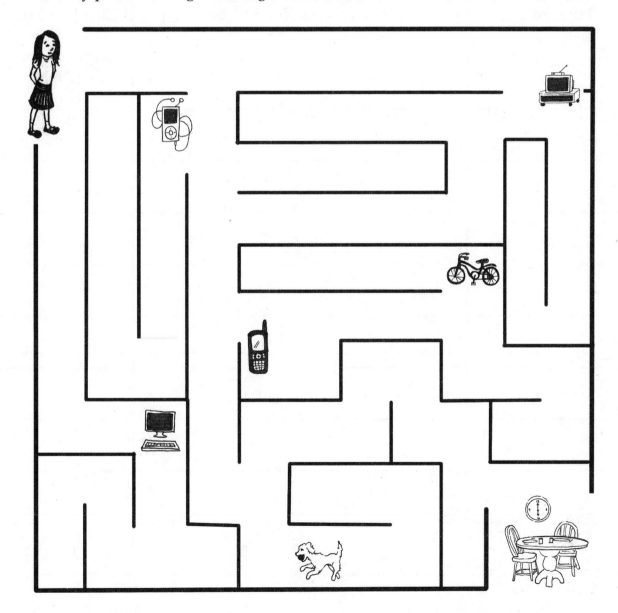

... And More to Do

On the chart below, write down the most important times you have to remember today. Tell where you have to be at each time. At the end of the day, put a check in the last column if you got to the right place at the right time.

Time of Day	Where You Need to Be	Check If You Got to the Right Place at the Right Time

---

For You to Know

Very few kids like doing homework, but homework helps you remember what you learned in class. If you didn't do some of your work at home, you might have to spend more time at school and maybe even go to school during the summer!

Haley was one of the best readers in her class, and she would read book after book at home, too. Every Saturday, she would take out four or five books from the library. Sometimes she read them all by Wednesday, and she'd ask her mom to make an extra trip to the library.

Math was another story. Haley wasn't good at math, and she particularly hated the worksheets she had to do outside of school. Lots of nights, Haley would do one or two problems from her homework and then stop. Rather than trying to solve the rest, she would just write in any old numbers, so it would look like she had finished.

When her teacher collected Haley's homework, he would shake his head. "I think we'd better have a talk with your parents," he told her one day. "You don't seem to be trying very hard at math, and if you don't try harder, you might get held back."

Haley was in quite a predicament.

What do you think would help Haley? Write it here:

_____

_____

_____

_____

For You to Do

Here are some things that kids say help them do their homework:

"I do my homework as soon as I get home from school. That gets it out of the way."

"I do my homework sitting next to my mom. She helps me when I need it."

"I used to have a hard time remembering my homework assignments, but now I use an audio recorder to remind me."

"I used to do my homework while I was watching TV, but it took forever. Now I turn off the TV, and it takes me just one hour."

"I do my homework in a special program after school."

Can you think of two things you could do differently to help you get your homework done? Write them below.

_____

_____

_____

_____

... *And More to Do*

Having a homework routine is the best way to make sure your homework gets done every day. Fill in the lines below to help you stay in a positive homework routine. You can make copies of this page to use for different days.

Write down when you will start: _____

Estimate how much time homework will take: _____

Assignment 1: _____

Assignment 2: _____

Assignment 3: _____

Assignment 4: _____

Write down what you will do when you need a break: _____

Write down who can help you if you need help: _____

Write down who will check your homework when it is complete: _____

Write down when you expect to finish: _____

What reward or treat can you give yourself after you get your homework done?

_____

You Can Take Better Care of Your Things

For You to Know

Lots of kids, and lots of adults too, have problems being organized. They don't put away their things and then they can't find them. It takes more time to look for something you misplaced than it does to put something away where it belongs when you are finished with it.

"We're going on a long car ride to see Uncle Joe," Ryan's mother told him one Saturday morning. "You might want to take your iPod or your Game Boy, or both."

Ryan didn't like the idea of a long ride, but he liked visiting his uncle, who had an awesome electric train set. He went to find his iPod; he looked under the bed, under the sofa cushions, and in his backpack, but it wasn't anywhere.

"I guess I'll just take my Game Boy," Ryan thought. It was on his desk, just where he had left it—but the battery wasn't charged! "Now where did I put that charger?" Ryan thought, and he looked all over his room, all over the living room, and all through his desk drawer. Had it disappeared into thin air?

Ryan thought about asking his mom or dad to help him find his iPod or charger, but he knew that they would be mad at him. So he decided he would just have to be bored on the long ride. And he was.

Do you ever misplace your things? Do you have a special place to keep your important things?

_____

_____

_____

_____

For You to Do

There's an old saying: "A place for everything and everything in its place." This saying tells us that it is important to be organized, to have just one place for each of our things, and to put things in their proper place when we are done using them. In the box below, draw a picture of Ryan's room after he learned to be follow this advice.

... And More to Do

Sometimes people use shoe boxes or other small boxes to sort things like handheld games, art or school supplies, or toys. Label the boxes below to show what you might put in each, and draw in things you might put in each box.

Ask your parents for some boxes to help you organize your things.

For You to Know

It is important to do certain things at certain times. You have to get ready for school on time, hand in your homework on time, wash up and brush your teeth on time, and go to bed on time. Adults don't like to keep reminding you of the things you need to do.

Robin's mother was always nagging her.

"Did you make your bed?" Robin's mother would ask.

"Did you brush your teeth?" Robin's mother would ask.

"Did you put away your toys?" Robin's mother would ask.

"Did you finish your reading assignment?" Robin's mother would ask.

When her mother asked these questions, most of the time Robin would say, "No, not yet."

What advice would you give Robin to keep her mother from nagging?

_____

_____

_____

_____

You Can Know What to Do Without Being Reminded

For You to Do

Lots of people use a "To Do" list to remind them of what they need to do during the day. Make photocopies of the To Do list below for each day of the week. Check each thing off when you have done it.

To Do List	
Things to Do Today	**Check Off When Each Thing Is Done**

... And More to Do

A calendar is another helpful way to keep track of what you have to do. On the calendar below, write in the things you have to do every day during this week. Check them off when you do them.

Monday	Tuesday	Wednesday	Thursday	Friday

Use this calendar for the things you have to do this weekend. Check them off when you do them.

Saturday	Sunday

Activity 19

You Can Ask for Help When You Need It

For You to Know

Some kids think they are bothering adults when they ask for help. Other kids simply forget that adults are there to help. And other kids may not realize when they need help. But it's important to ask for help when you need it.

Will was always in trouble for not doing his homework. His mother said, "I'm tired of reminding you about your homework. If you can't do it by yourself, you'll just have to do it at school."

That night, Will watched his favorite TV program. Then he sat down at his computer to start his homework, but instead, he went to a website he liked and played some games. His mother didn't remind him to finish his homework, so he didn't.

The next day, when Will's teacher asked everyone to turn in their homework, Will didn't have anything to hand in. He knew he would be in trouble by the end of the day.

Who could Will have asked for help when he realized there was a problem? What could he have said?

_____

_____

_____

_____

For You to Do

It is important to remember that everyone needs help at some time. Do you know a carpenter? Someone had to help him learn to use his tools. Do you know a good basketball player? Someone had to help her learn to dribble, shoot, and guard other players.

Different people can help you with different things. Next to each picture below, write down who could help you learn to use that object. Try to think of as many different people as you can.

... *And More to Do*

Everyone you know who is good at something learned to ask for help. Think of three people you admire, and ask each to answer these questions:

- What is something you needed help with when you were my age?

- What is something you need help with now?

- How do you know when you need help and when you should just try to do something on your own?

- Has anyone ever told you that they wouldn't help you?

Write down what you learned about asking for help:

_____

_____

_____

_____

_____

For You to Know

Some kids are grouchy in the morning, while others start to melt down in the afternoon. Some kids with ADHD have problems doing certain tasks, like math homework or chores, but can play video games for hours and never get distracted or bored. If you have problems at certain times of the day or when you do certain tasks, you need to know when to take a break and how to refocus yourself.

Paul was pretty easygoing—at least in the morning. He got up for school, ate breakfast, and gathered his books and homework, all with a big smile on his face. Mornings at school were nearly always good. Paul liked everything on the schedule: reading, social studies, art, and recess.

But most afternoons were not so good for him. In the afternoon, Paul had math, science, and silent reading. He didn't like math or science and was tired by then, so he found it hard to concentrate on reading. By two o'clock each day, Paul couldn't wait for school to end, and that is when he usually did things that got him into trouble. He would talk to Benny, who had the desk next to his. Or he would start doodling or just stare out the window.

His teacher would stand right over Paul, frowning, and point to the work that Paul should be doing. Paul didn't like that at all. He would try to concentrate, but it was very hard to do.

Do you have a time of day that is hard for you? How about a particular subject?

_____

_____

_____

_____

You Can Know When You Need a Break

For You to Do

When you find your mind wandering, or you feel fidgety or so tired that you can hardly keep your eyes open, it's time for a break. Taking a break will help you feel more alert and better able to concentrate on your work.

Paul thought of several ways to take a break in school, but some of his ideas weren't as good as others. Circle the ideas that are helpful ways for Paul—and you—to take a break.

The ADHD Workbook for Kids

... And More to Do

Make photocopies of the shapes below and cut them out. In each, draw or write a helpful way to take a break. Then use each as a bookmark to help remind you of good ways to refocus yourself.

Activity 21

You Can Handle Days When Everything Seems to Go Wrong

For You to Know

Some days are harder than others. There are days when everything seems to go wrong. You may get yelled at by a teacher or picked on by another kid, or you may lose something important. But even the hardest days are easier when you learn have a positive attitude about yourself and those around you.

Keisha was trying to fall asleep, but she kept thinking about her day. It had been really awful.

She had known it was going to rain but forgot her umbrella and got drenched. Her backpack wasn't closed all the way, so her homework got soaked, and her teacher got mad at her for being so careless.

Her best friend, Heidi, had a stomach bug and threw up in front of the whole class. Keisha started to feel like she had to vomit, too, but she didn't.

Then she got a C- on her science quiz, even though she had studied very hard. She was sure her mom would be mad at her. When she got off the school bus at home, she tripped and scraped her knee. She slammed the door behind her, and her mother yelled at her for slamming the door.

"What a day!" Keisha thought. "Could things get any worse?"

Have you ever had a day like Keisha's? What happened? How did you make it better?

_____

_____

_____

_____

For You to Do

A positive attitude is very important for coping with difficult days. If you have a negative attitude, you

- think that things will always be difficult;

- blame other people for your problems;

- see things as worse than they really are;

- don't pay attention to the good things in your life;

- think that other people have all the control in your life;

- think that everyone is picking on you.

But if you have a positive attitude, you

- understand that even difficult problems can be solved;

- take responsibility for your problems and try to find good solutions;

- appreciate the things in your life that are good;

- try to find out why things are going wrong and how to make them better;

- have hope that things will get better;

- do the best you can, no matter what anyone else thinks.

These three kids are having problems that kids with ADHD often have. Write a positive statement that each one could be thinking.

... *And More to Do*

Write down some problems you had this week. For each, write a negative way to think about the problem. Then write a positive statement you could say to yourself.

Problem	Negative Attitude	Positive Statement

For You to Know

Lots of kids worry about taking tests. Sometimes worrying about taking tests is worse than the test itself! But there are simple things you can learn to make your studying and test-taking more successful.

Jonathon had read all the chapters in his textbook and answered all the questions on the practice worksheets, but he was still worried about taking his earth science test.

"How do I know what questions will be on the test?" he asked his mother. "We covered a million things, and I can't remember them all."

"You just have to study in an organized way," his mother said. "Write down the most important things you learned and concentrate on those. I'll show you." She spread out all his homework assignments, took a yellow marker, and showed Jonathon how to highlight what was important. She told Jonathon to look back in his science book and see if he had learned about other things that were important. Then she helped him make a list of all the facts that might be on the test. Jonathon read the list over and over, and then his mother asked him questions about each fact.

By the test day, Jonathon was ready. He had not only learned a lot about earth science, but also how to study! He felt pretty smart.

Do you know any important tricks to help you prepare for tests? Write them here:

_____

_____

_____

_____

For You to Do

If you have trouble with tests, there are some important things you can do to improve your grades, but they have to be done in the right order. Using a pencil, write a 1 next to the first thing to be done, a 2 next to the second thing to be done, and so on.

_____ Know what you are being tested on.

_____ Get all of your study material together.

_____ Understand the format of the test. Will it be multiple choice, true or false, essay, or some other form?

_____ Listen carefully to the directions to the test.

_____ Take good notes.

_____ Make sure you work fast enough to finish the test.

_____ If you skip questions, make sure you leave enough time to go back to the ones you skipped.

_____ Check your answers.

_____ After the test has been corrected, learn from your mistakes by reviewing it with your teacher or parent.

_____ Ask for help with things you don't understand.

... And More to Do

Now that you know the things that will help you take tests, write them in the correct order in the chart below. Use this chart when you take your next test. Check off each test-taking tip when you have used it.

Test-Taking Tip	Check When Used

Section III
Making and Keeping Friends

Kids with ADHD are usually fun to be with. Most have plenty of energy to play or to do sports, and they have lots of ideas about things to do. But some behaviors that go along with ADHD may make it hard to have good friends. Kids with ADHD often forget the importance of listening to others or taking into account what other kids want to do. Some kids with ADHD have trouble remembering the rules, or they may not like the rules and want to change them. Other kids with ADHD get bored more quickly than their friends, and then they may argue about what to do.

Making good friends is an important part of growing up. The activities in this section will help you find good friends and will also help you deal with kids who don't want to be friends with you.

For You to Know

Kids with ADHD can act a little different from other kids. Sometimes they get teased for talking too fast or talking too loudly or being too hyper. But kids with ADHD aren't the only ones who get teased. Many kids get teased because they are a little different, and all kids need to know when teasing is really harmful and should be reported.

Josh liked to play with the other kids at school, but they didn't seem to like to play with him. At recess, when Josh wanted to join their kickball game, someone would always say, "We have enough players already."

So Josh would find things to do by himself. He would throw a ball into the air and then chase it down. He would hang from the jungle gym and make monkey faces. Sometimes he would just walk around the playground looking at other kids, and when they looked back, he would salute.

"You know, you're really weird?" Allyson said to Josh one day. Josh didn't know what to say back. Another day Josh brushed against Jose on the cafeteria line. "Get your cooties off me!" Jose said. Josh's feelings were hurt, but he just walked away.

Josh wasn't actually teased every day, but sometimes he felt like he was. He would often ask his mother if he could stay home. But of course she wouldn't let him.

Did you ever ask for help when someone was teasing you? Tell what happened.

_____

_____

_____

_____

For You to Do

Some teasing is not that serious, but other teasing is very harmful. Use a blue crayon to color the teasing that is not serious. Use a yellow crayon for the teasing that is pretty mean and a red crayon for the teasing that is very harmful.

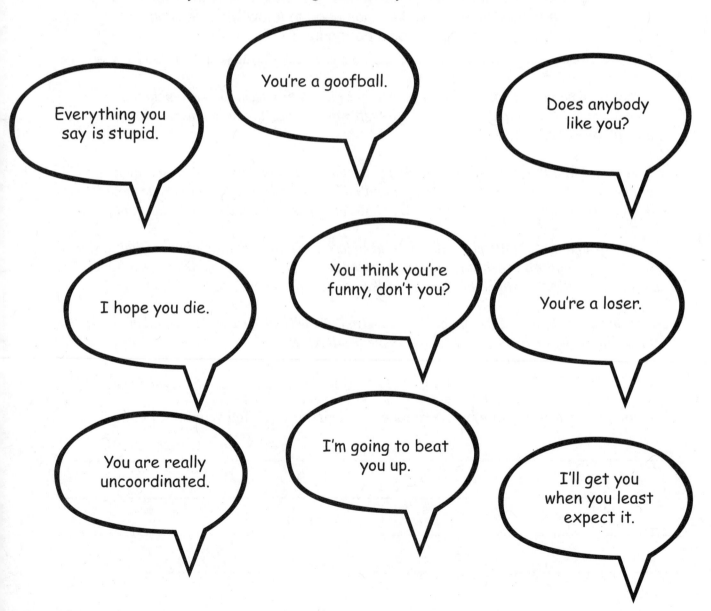

... *And More to Do*

In these empty balloons, write in some things that kid have teased you about. Color them in as you did before, using blue, yellow, and red crayons.

Show this exercise to an adult and talk about what you can do when you are teased a little or a lot.

Helping Children Gain Self-Confidence, Social Skills, and Self-Control

For You to Know

Everyone gets angry at some time, but if you get angry a lot of the time, it's important to find out why. Also, if you express your anger in ways that upset other people (by screaming, throwing tantrums, destroying things, hurting people, and so on), you have to find better ways to express yourself.

Alicia couldn't stand her little sister, Frieda. Frieda was such a pain! When Alicia had a friend over, Frieda had to hang around them. Alicia would scream at her to get lost, but then Alicia would get into trouble. Because Frieda was such a pest, Alicia was always in a bad mood.

Once when Alicia thought she had too much homework, she threw her book bag out their apartment window. Of course, she was punished. Once when her mother made spinach, Alicia said loudly, "I hate spinach," and she spit onto her plate. She was punished for that, too.

One morning when Frieda was annoying her, Alicia slammed her bedroom door. Her father knocked, then came in and asked, "Why are you so mad all the time?"

Alicia answered, "Because I hate living here! Everyone is against me."

"No one is against you—" her father began, but Alicia got up and ran out of the room. Whenever someone talked to Alicia about her attitude or behavior, she didn't want to listen.

How often do you get angry? What do you do when you are angry?

_____

_____

_____

_____

For You to Do

Everyone gets angry sometimes, but not everyone knows how to control their anger. For some kids, anger seems to control them. Look at the list of things that some kids do when they are angry. Five of these ways to deal with anger are helpful; five are not. Circle the ones that are helpful.

Scream as loud as you can.

Take ten deep breaths to calm yourself.

Suggest several solutions to the problem that is making you mad.

Play a trick or practical joke on the person you are mad at.

Sit in a comfortable chair, relax all of your muscles, and breathe deeply for a few minutes.

Hold your feelings in and don't tell anyone what is wrong.

Draw a mean picture of the person who made you angry and give it to him or her.

Do something to distract yourself from your anger.

Think of a way to make the person you are angry at even madder than you are.

Talk about what is bothering you.

... And More to Do

Write down five things that get you angry. Next to each, write down a good way to deal with your anger.

What Makes You Angry?	Good Ways to Deal with Your Anger

For You to Know

Everyone has different feelings at times, but some feelings are harder to talk about than others. Some kids find it hard to tell people when they are angry. Some kids find it hard to talk about being sad. When you are jealous or guilty or embarrassed, you may find it hard to talk about your feelings, but talking about them almost always helps you feel better.

Many of the kids Connor knew came from wealthy families. Sometimes he fibbed so that his friends wouldn't think his family was poor. When Nick got a new iPod, Connor said, "I'm getting one for my birthday—the expensive kind with lots of memory." At Lilli's pool party, Connor said, "We're getting a pool too, like yours, except maybe bigger." But Connor's family didn't have the money for a pool.

Connor told so many fibs like these that he was afraid to invite any of the kids in his class to his house. They would see right away that his family was not well off. He felt guilty about lying to his friends and embarrassed to tell his parents what he had done. And he was a little angry because his family didn't have any extra money to spend on the things he liked.

Although he wasn't sure who he was mad at, Connor didn't know what to do or say.

If you were Connor, what would you do? Who can you talk to when you feel upset?

_____

_____

_____

_____

For You to Do

Talking about your feelings becomes easier with practice. This game is called Feelings Toss. Try playing it with someone you trust to understand your feelings, like a parent, a good friend, a teacher, or a counselor. Before you play, make a copy of the game sheet and get twenty pennies.

1. Put a copy of the game sheet on a flat table.

2. Stand about an arm's length from the game sheet.

3. Toss a penny and try to get it into a feelings circle. If the penny is more than half in the circle, you get the number of points shown. You then talk about a time you had that feeling.

4. Then it's the other player's turn. Play continues until all the pennies have been used.

5. Total the points; the person who has the most points is the winner.

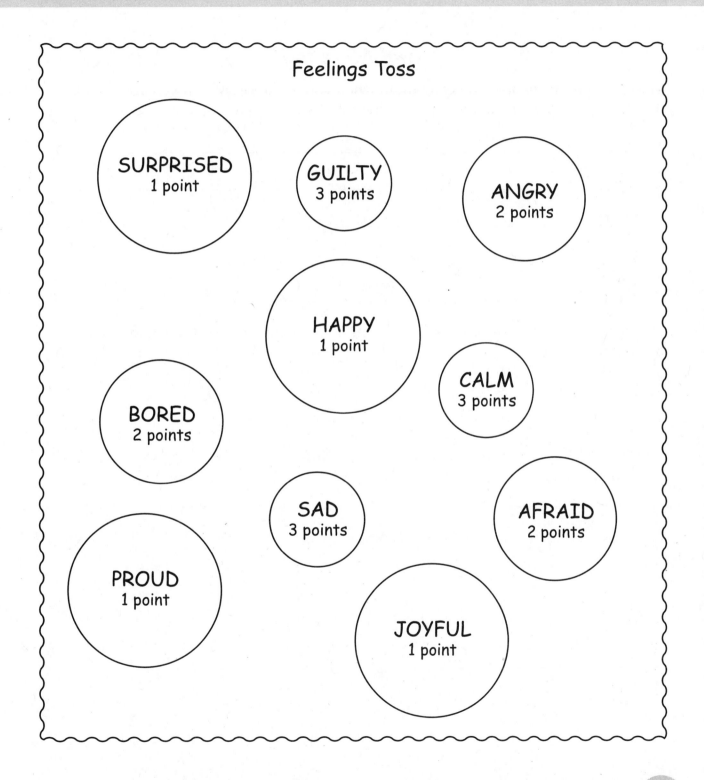

Feelings Toss

SURPRISED
1 point

GUILTY
3 points

ANGRY
2 points

HAPPY
1 point

CALM
3 points

BORED
2 points

SAD
3 points

AFRAID
2 points

PROUD
1 point

JOYFUL
1 point

Helping Children Gain Self-Confidence, Social Skills, and Self-Control

... And More to Do

Make a list of the people you can talk to when you are upset. When you are feeling upset, try to talk to one of these people by the end of the day.

1. _____

2. _____

3. _____

4. _____

5. _____

Do you need to add more people to this list? Is there anyone else you could talk to when you are upset?

For You to Know

Being popular just means that most kids like you and few kids dislike you. All kids want to be popular, but sometimes they don't really understand what it takes. Some kids think that you have to wear certain clothes or listen to a certain type of music or be good at sports to be popular. But in reality, kids like other kids who are kind, helpful, and considerate of others.

Everyone seemed to like Aisha. She was smart and cute, but certainly not the smartest or cutest girl in her class. But she was the girl everyone wanted to play with at recess and on weekends. She also had lots of interests: ballet, tennis, art, reading, movies, and more. Her only problem was not having enough time in the week to do all her activities and also spend time with her friends.

Bailey was not as well liked as Aisha, although she wanted to be. But Bailey had a few bad habits that annoyed some of the other kids in her class. For example, Bailey was very competitive, and when she played games, she always wanted to win. If she didn't win, she sometimes accused other kids of cheating or being unfair. Some kids also thought that Bailey had an attitude. She would ignore anyone she didn't like, even turning her back while that person was talking.

Because of the way she acted, Bailey didn't spend a lot of time with other kids. When she asked girls to come over, they would usually say they were busy.

Do you know kids like Aisha? Do you know kids like Bailey? Who are you more like?

_____

_____

_____

_____

You Can Help Yourself Be Well Liked

For You to Do

Kids who are popular usually have lots of good personal qualities. They are thoughtful, fair, and always aware of other kids' feelings. Write down what the kids on the right might be saying that would make them well liked.

The ADHD Workbook for Kids

... And More to Do

One of the simplest things you can do to be well liked is to be helpful. You don't have to be helpful to anyone in particular; just be helpful whenever you can to anyone who would benefit from kindness. You may be surprised at how quickly people start treating you differently.

Try to do something helpful for someone every day for two weeks. Write down what you do below.

Day 1 _____

Day 2 _____

Day 3 _____

Day 4 _____

Day 5 _____

Day 6 _____

Day 7 _____

Day 8 _____

Day 9 _____

Day 10 _____

Day 11 _____

Day 12 _____

Day 13 _____

Day 14 _____

You Can Understand How Other Kids Feel

For You to Know

To get along with others, it is important to understand what other kids are feeling. Sometimes adults say, "You have to put yourself in another person's shoes." There is also a word for understanding another person's feelings or point of view: "empathy." When you have empathy, you treat people differently than if you don't understand how they are feeling. Good friends always have empathy for each other.

Jacob had just moved to a new town and still hadn't made any friends. He was starting school in a week, and he was worried about whether kids would be nice to him. "What if everyone just ignores me?" Jacob asked his father.

"What would you do if you were in a school and a new kid came into your classroom?" his father answered.

Jacob thought, then said, "Well, I would be nice to him. I would say hello and ask him how he liked the school. I might ask him over to play."

"Well, that's probably how most of the kids will treat you," Jacob's father said. "The best way to think about how other people will act is to think how you would act if you were in the same situation.

"But not everyone acts in the same way, because people are different," Jacob's father went on. "Some kids may be shy and won't say hello right away. There will probably be some kids who are not as nice as you, and they may not pay any attention to you at all. You can't know how other kids will act until you meet them, but if you understand that everyone is different and has different feelings, it will be easier to make new friends."

Have you ever been in a situation like Jacob's? What happened?

_____

_____

_____

_____

For You to Do

It is always helpful when other people tell you how they are feeling. When they do, you will probably know just how to act. But many times kids don't tell you how they are feeling, and you have to figure it out for yourself.

Draw a line from each child to the correct feeling. The answers are upside down at the bottom of the page.

1.
Angry

2.
Frustrated

3.
Sad

4.
Guilty

1. Sad 2. Angry 3. Guilty 4. Frustrated

... And More to Do

You can learn to be a "feelings detective." Turn on the TV and find a show that you have never seen before. (You might need to ask your parent's permission before you do this.) Now turn off the sound and see if you can figure out what people are feeling just by their facial expressions, their body language, and what they are doing. In the chart below, write down what you see.

What You See	Feelings

For You to Know

Some kids want to have fun with other kids and have friends to do things with, but they spend a lot of their time alone. It is hard for some kids to find good friends, but it will be easier if you learn the important rules of making and keeping good friends.

Risa was taller than all the kids in her class, probably because she had been held back a year when she was in kindergarten. She was a good reader, but she had some learning problems along with her ADHD, and she went to the Resource Room several times a week.

But Risa's biggest problem was her crying. She would cry if she got frustrated doing her schoolwork. She would cry if she tripped and bumped her knee. She would cry if another kid was the least bit mean to her. Sometimes no one really knew why Risa was crying, but she cried in class almost every other day.

Her crying made it hard for Risa to have friends. The other kids thought she was babyish. They didn't invite her to play during recess because they thought she would just end up in tears. Her only friend, Eva, was a "sometimes" friend: sometimes Eva would want to be with Risa and sometimes she wouldn't even say hello to her.

Risa was very lonely and hated going to school. She told her mother that she wanted to move to another state or at least to another school. But Risa's mother had another idea. "There are lots of kids who aren't in your class or even your school. Let's see if we can find some other places where you might meet new friends," her mother suggested.

Where do you think Risa could meet new friends? Other than school, where do you meet new friends?

_____

_____

_____

_____

For You to Do

Most of the time, kids who are friends have lots in common. They might like the same TV shows and music and the same sports or activities. The best way to find new friends is to think about what you are like and what you like to do, and then try to find kids who are like you. What you write down below can help you think about yourself and the things you will look for in a friend.

Write down three things you like to do on weekends.

1. _____

2. _____

3. _____

Write down three things you don't like to do with other kids.

1. _____

2. _____

3. _____

Write down your three favorite singers or bands.

1. _____

2. _____

3. _____

Write down a hobby you have or want to take up.

_____

Write down something really important about yourself.

_____

What is your favorite activity to do with a group of kids?

_____

What are your favorite books?

_____

What is something you'd like to do but have never done?

_____

... And More to Do

Now that you have found out some of the things you might have in common with a good friend, it is time to think about where you might meet a friend who is a lot like you. Write down five places where you might find someone who is similar to you.

1. _____

2. _____

3. _____

4. _____

5. _____

For You to Know

It is great to have special friends, but it is also important to know how to have fun with just about anybody. It isn't hard to get along with other kids as long as you remember some simple social rules.

Robert's parents were putting him in private school, and he was going to have to learn to make new friends. But he had no idea how to do this.

"I've had the same friends since I was three years old," Robert said to his dad. "How can I just start over?"

"Being a good friend is like riding a bike," his father said. "Once you've learned how to do it, you never forget. You have lots of friends because you're fun to be with and you're funny, too. I see you with your friends, and they're always happy to be with you. So just be yourself, and you won't have any trouble making friends."

Robert thought about his father's advice, but he wasn't so sure it would work.

What do you think is the secret to making friends?

_____

_____

_____

_____

For You to Do

There are many social rules that will help you get along well with other kids, and you have probably heard them all before. But knowing the rules is not the same as following them.

To find out how good you are at following social rules, rate each of these statements on a scale from 1 to 3, where 1 = never, 2 = sometimes, and 3 = most of the time. You can ask a parent or another adult, like a teacher or counselor, to rate you as well.

_____ I take turns when playing games.

_____ I play games fairly.

_____ I share my things with other kids.

_____ I talk things over when there is a problem.

_____ I wait my turn when other people are talking.

_____ I am considerate of other people's feelings.

_____ I tell other kids what I like about them.

_____ I am polite.

_____ I ask if I can play before joining a group of other kids.

_____ I show respect for other people's things.

The higher your score, the better you are at following social rules and the easier it will be to make friends.

... And More to Do

Look over your ratings. If you have asked adults to rate you, look over their answers and compare them with yours. Write down the top three social rules you need to work on.

1. _____

2. _____

3. _____

Ask a parent or other adult to act out situations where you can practice following these rules.

> ## For You to Know
>
> Having a best friend is very important. A best friend is someone you can do things with that you both enjoy. A best friend is someone you can talk to almost every day. A best friend is someone who will always be there when you need him or her.

Ethan had lots of energy. He would wake up ready to play a game or ride his bike or go on an adventure. The problem was that Ethan didn't have anyone special to do these things with. He knew a lot of kids, but he wasn't really close friends with any of them.

More than anything, Ethan wanted to be best friends with Micah. Micah was very funny. He was a really good basketball player, and Ethan loved basketball. He lived only two blocks from Ethan, but they never played together.

One Saturday, Ethan had nothing to do and he complained to his mother that he was bored.

"Why don't you call Micah?" his mother asked. "You always say you like him, but you never invite him over."

"But I don't know if he likes me," Ethan said. "What if he doesn't like me and he won't come over?"

"Well, you can't find out if you don't ask," Ethan's mother said. "And even if Micah is busy today, you can ask him another time. Think of something that you both like to do, and ask Micah to come over and do it with you."

"We both like basketball, " Ethan said, "but Micah has lots of other friends who play basketball with him."

"You can find lots of excuses to not call Micah," Ethan's mother said, "but you'll never know if he'll be a good friend until you give him a call."

"Okay," Ethan said. "I'll think about it."

If you were Ethan, would you call Micah? What do you think he would say?

_____

_____

_____

_____

For You to Do

There are lots of things you can do to have a best friend. Here are just a few:

- Talk to your friend about things you are both interested in.

- Be a good listener. Don't interrupt when your friend is talking.

- Compliment your friend about things you admire. Everyone enjoys a compliment.

- Take turns with your friend, whether you are picking out activities or playing a game.

- Pay attention to your friend's feelings. If you don't know what he or she is feeling, ask.

- Be flexible about your needs. Always be willing to compromise.

- Include other people in your friendship. Lots of things are more fun when they are done in a group.

- Don't hold grudges. If your friend does something wrong or says the wrong thing, tell that friend how you feel and then let it go.

The most important thing you can do to have a best friend is to do things together. In the space below, write down five things you like to do with a friend:

1. _____

2. _____

3. _____

4. _____

5. _____

... And More to Do

If you don't have a best friend yet, there is one thing you have to do—be friendly! This may sound strange, but being friendly is the simplest way to get other kids to like you and to want to spend time with you. So how do you "be friendly"? It's easy. Smile at people. Say hello. Offer to help out whenever you can. Share your things. Be kind and considerate.

And the most important things you can do is to look friendly. Practice looking in the mirror and saying hello to yourself in different ways. You may feel a bit goofy at first, but give it a try.

Now look through an old magazine. Cut out three to five pictures of kids who look friendly and paste them below. Next to each picture, write down the things that make this kid look friendly.

For You to Know

Some kids like to goof around. Some kids like to play jokes on other kids. Some kids like to do rude things to get other kids to laugh. It's fun to make other people laugh, but not when your jokes or behavior might hurt someone's feelings.

Anthony was considered the class clown. He would do just about anything to make other kids laugh. But his jokes and stunts often got Anthony into trouble.

His teacher had a limp, and one time Anthony imitated her by pretending to limp around the playground. Another teacher saw him and sent him to the principal's office. In the cafeteria one day, Anthony said, "This stew looks like throw-up" and made some awful vomiting noises. The lunch aide told him that his behavior was "inappropriate," and she made him sit by himself. Anthony also liked to repeat his older brother's jokes. But many of those jokes made fun of people, and his teacher told him that they were "trash" jokes that belong in the trash can.

Anthony liked to go to school because he liked to entertain the kids in his class, but his grades weren't very good. His teacher told his parents: "Anthony is a smart boy, and if he spent half the time trying to learn that he does trying to be a clown, he would be my best pupil." Anthony's parents thought that his behavior in school was nothing to laugh at.

Do you think you are funny? What would your friends say?

_____

_____

_____

_____

For You to Do

Humor is an important part of being with your friends. And laughing is good for you, too! Scientists have found that laughing can help you calm down when you are stressed and get better faster when you are sick. But certain kinds of humor make you feel worse, not better.

Take these kids, for example. Which kids do you think were funny, and which ones went too far? Check the sentences that describe kids who went too far with their attempts to be funny.

_____ Billy said his sister's haircut made her look like a clown, and then he imitated a clown he had seen on television.

_____ Shaina put fake vomit in her father's briefcase.

_____ Meghan made up a silly song about her friend Troy that made him seem like he was really dumb. She stood where Troy could hear her and sang it to another friend.

_____ When his teacher left the room, Chris stood on his desk and tried to juggle three books.

_____ Tanya told a joke that made fun of people with blonde hair.

_____ Liam made farting noises in the school cafeteria.

How many sentences did you check? If you checked all of them, you were correct. All these kids went too far with their humor. Their jokes and stunts could have hurt someone's feelings or gotten them into trouble.

You Can Be Funny Without Hurting Anyone's Feelings

... And More to Do

People often look funny in photographs. But a photograph can be even funnier when you add something weird the person could be thinking or saying. With a parent's permission, make copies of photographs of three people you know. Using the copies, cut out the faces and paste them below these speech and thought balloons. Then write in something each person could be thinking or saying that is funny, but not mean. For more fun, you can make copies of this page and do this activity with a friend or family member.

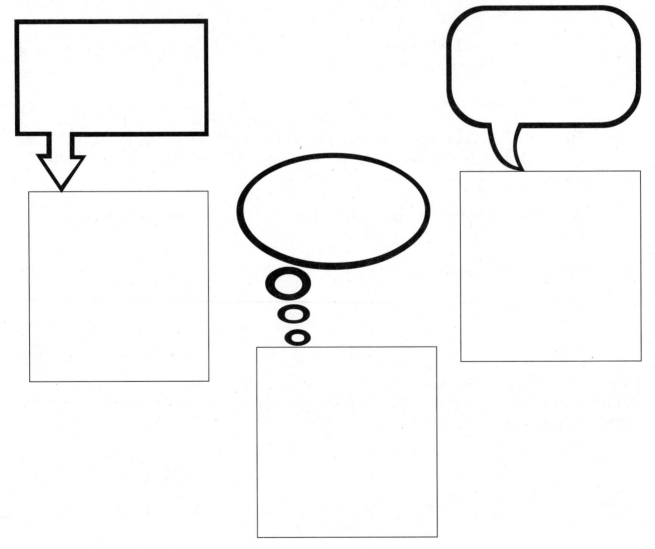

For You to Know

It's important to stick up for your rights. If someone teases you, you have to tell that person to stop. If someone takes something that belongs to you, you should try to get it back, and if that is difficult, you should tell an adult. No one has the right to hurt you in any way.

Abigail was the chubbiest girl in her school. Her mother said Abigail had a medical problem that made it hard for her to lose weight even if she always chose healthful foods. And Abigail didn't like eating that way. She would rather have an oversized cookie or two scoops of ice cream. Her mother said, "You can have all the vegetables you want," but Abigail didn't really like vegetables; she liked sweets.

Kids often made fun of Abigail behind her back and even to her face. They would call her "fatty" or "chub-o," and of course she felt very hurt.

Abigail was not as good at sports as the other kids. She was a slow runner and quickly got tired. One day during gym class, while they were picking teams, a snotty girl named Patricia said to Abigail, "You might as well stay in the back because you're going to be the last one picked anyway." And Patricia pointed to the back of the gym.

But Abigail knew that she didn't have to listen to what Patricia said. She stood tall, looked Patricia in the eye, and said, "I'll stand wherever I want, Patricia. I have as much right to get picked as you do."

Patricia was shocked. She had expected Abigail to just walk away. "Whatever," Patricia said—and she was the one who walked away.

Has another child ever told you to do something you didn't want to do? What did you do?

_____

_____

_____

_____

For You to Do

When kids stick up for their rights, we say they are being assertive. Being assertive means standing up for yourself, but not being aggressive. Insulting someone back or threatening them or even fighting with them is not a good solution to being picked on. Instead, just do these five things:

1. Stand up straight.

2. Look the person in the eye.

3. State your rights in a calm, clear voice that is not too soft and not too loud.

4. If the person who is bothering you continues to do the same thing, state your rights over and over again. Do not say anything else.

5. If the person threatens you in any way, walk away. If you are worried that the person might harm you in some way, immediately tell an adult.

Kids sometimes say things like this to be mean. Write in what you would say back. The first two assertive responses have been written in for you.

You can't play with us. You're too stupid.	*I'll find other kids to play with. I don't like it when you call me names.*
Give me your dessert.	*I'm not going to give you something that belongs to me.*
You can't sit here. Go sit somewhere else.	
Be quiet. No one wants to hear what you think.	
Where did you get your clothes—the dump?	
Don't you know you're not wanted around here?	

... And More to Do

When people are assertive, their body language tells others that they are serious about what they are saying. Look at the two kids below. The girl looks confident and sure of herself. The boy looks unsure and afraid. Make a list of all the differences you see in their body language. The answers are upside down on the bottom of the page.

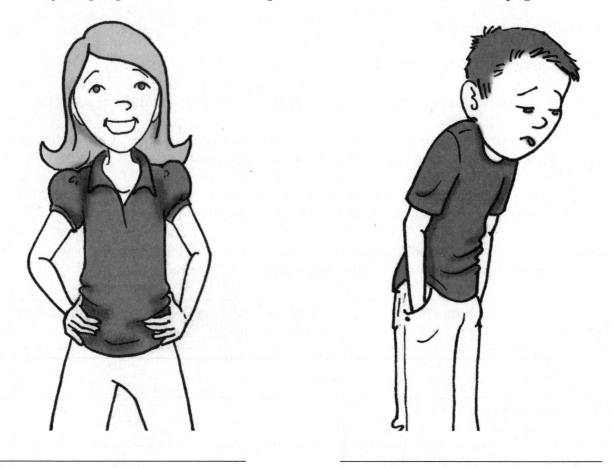

_____

_____

_____

Boy: slouches; looks worried; doesn't make eye contact

Girl: stands up straight; has confident expression; makes eye contact

---

For You to Know

Everyone argues sometimes, but some kids seem to argue all the time, particularly some brothers and sisters. Too much arguing, whether at home or school, is always a problem. If you argue a lot, you will be much happier when you learn how to compromise and avoid fights.

Kevin and his younger sister, Sonya, argued all the time. They argued about what TV show to watch. They argued about the temperature in the room. They argued about whether the car window should be open or shut. It seemed there was nothing they agreed on.

Of course, their parents were not happy with all the arguing. "You have to learn to compromise," their father said. "If I hear just one more argument, you'll both be punished. I'll start by taking away your allowances, and if that doesn't work, your TV and computer privileges. And if that doesn't work, I'll find something else to take away. I mean it, no more arguing!"

Kevin and Sonya had never seen their father so serious. But how were they going to start compromising when they had never ever done it before?

Fortunately, their mom had an answer. "There are lots of ways to compromise," she said, "but for now, let's do something simple. Whenever you disagree, take turns on who gets what they want. Sonya will get the first turn because she's the youngest. Then it is Kevin's turn, then back to Sonya, and so on. Kevin, you have to keep a notebook and write down whose turn it is whenever you have a disagreement. Okay?"

"Okay," Kevin said, but he thought it was unfair that he had to keep track of whose turn it was.

"Okay," said Sonya, but she didn't trust Kevin to keep track of the turns.

Do you think this solution will work? What might go wrong?

_____

_____

_____

_____

For You to Do

When two people compromise, each gives in a little, and they come up with a solution that fits both people's needs. A compromise isn't a perfect solution, but it is good enough that both people who disagree are satisfied. The more you learn to compromise, the easier it will be to get along with your friends and family. For each of these disagreements, write a compromise for Kevin and Sonya.

Kevin says ...	Sonya says ...	Their Compromise
I want to watch the Batman movie.	I want to watch cartoons.	
I want our family to go to the beach.	I want our family to go on a picnic.	
I want to eat macaroni and cheese.	I want to eat hot dogs.	
I want to use the bathroom first.	I want to use the bathroom first.	

... And More to Do

Write down two problems you are having with other kids or family members. For each problem, write down a compromise. Show your compromises to a parent or other adult and ask what they think of them.

Problem: _____

_____

_____

Compromise: _____

_____

_____

_____

Problem: _____

_____

_____

Compromise: _____

_____

_____

_____

Section IV
Feeling Good About Yourself

Having ADHD can be difficult at times. But it is helpful to remember that almost everyone has problems at some time. Nobody has the "perfect" life.

Unlike some problems, ADHD can get you into trouble at home and at school. Even when adults and kids know that you have ADHD, they may sometimes lose their patience, criticize you, or even punish you for certain behaviors. Getting into trouble with other people can lead to another problem, one that can be even more serious than ADHD. If people keep telling you that you are doing something wrong, you may start to feel that there is something wrong with you. And that simply isn't true.

The activities in this section will help you see that having ADHD is a problem you can learn to live with and can even be seen as a special gift. You can learn to control the problem behaviors that come with ADHD and show the world all the things that make you special.

You Can Be Different and Still Be Accepted

For You to Know

Some kids with ADHD have to go to the nurse's office to take medication. Some kids with ADHD get help in a learning center or from a classroom aide. Some kids with ADHD have special accommodations at school. Everyone in the world has something that makes them different, and being different doesn't mean that there is something wrong with you.

There was once a young boy who had many problems at school. He didn't like being there because he was bored a lot of the time. He liked to daydream during class, and his teachers often got mad at him for that. As he got older, this boy started to skip school. Instead of going to school, he would go to see movies. That got him into even more trouble. This boy's name was Walt Disney, the creator of Mickey Mouse, Donald Duck, Disney World, and Disneyland.

Did anyone ever call you a dreamer? What do you daydream about?

_____

_____

_____

_____

For You to Do

There is a long list of famous people who say they have ADHD, including actors Danny Glover and Robin Williams, Olympic swimmer Michael Phelps, and businessman Charles Schwab. Choose one of these people to learn more about, and write about what you have found out. If you like, you can choose another famous person who has ADHD.

_____

_____

_____

_____

_____

_____

_____

_____

_____

_____

_____

... And More to Do

Some people say that ADHD is a gift, not a problem. Kids with ADHD tend to be very creative and curious and to solve problems in original ways. They are often passionate (have strong positive feelings) about their interests. These descriptions might fit you, or you might have other differences that make you very special.

In the frame on the left, draw something about yourself that makes you really special. Then think of something you are passionate about that might make you famous some day. Draw yourself doing this thing in the frame on the right.

Activity 35   You Can Recognize Your Special Gifts

For You to Know

Kids with ADHD often have special talents. They often have great imaginations, lots of enthusiasm, and really interesting ways of looking at problems.

Taima's mother said that she was born full of mischief. When she was a toddler, she would empty cereal boxes onto the floor, then roll in the cereal. When she got older, she would wander off when her mother wasn't looking and explore the nearby woods. At school, Taima had a hard time paying attention because she liked to daydream about inventions she could build, like a garbage launcher to catapult garbage into outer space. Taima had ideas for inventions almost every day, and she liked to draw them in a notebook right away so she wouldn't forget them. But then she usually had to stay after school to finish the work she hadn't completed in class.

When her teacher, Mrs. Willis, saw Taima's notebook of inventions, she was very impressed. "These are wonderful," Mrs. Willis said. "Not only are your ideas great, but your drawings are amazing. I want to show them to our art teacher. I bet you she'll want to put you in the class for kids who are artistically talented. You still need to concentrate on your regular work," Mrs. Willis continued, "but I also want to make sure you have time to develop your special talent."

Taima was so proud of herself, all she could do was smile and say, "Thank you Mrs. Willis."

Do you have a special talent that no one appreciates? How can you get attention for this special talent?

_____

_____

_____

_____

You Can Recognize Your Special Gifts

For You to Do

Do you have the gift of imagination? See if you can draw something special in the four boxes here and on the next page.

Draw a picture of yourself winning a prize.

Draw a picture of yourself as a superhero. Make sure to show your superpowers.

Draw a picture of an invention that nobody has thought of before.

Draw a picture of yourself doing something special ten years from now.

... And More to Do

Write down ten things that make you special. If you can't think of ten, ask your parents or teachers what they think makes you special.

1. _____

2. _____

3. _____

4. _____

5. _____

6. _____

7. _____

8. _____

9. _____

10. _____

For You to Know

Some people think that certain chemicals in food can make kids with ADHD more hyper and make it harder for them to concentrate. Many people think that ADHD can be helped by eating a healthy diet. Pretty much everyone agrees that a healthy diet includes a balance of protein, whole grains, vegetables, and fruit, with minimum of sweets and junk food.

Richard was a very skinny baby and toddler, so his parents never worried that he would eat too much. In fact, his mother worried that he was too thin, so she would give him high-calorie food that would help him put on weight.

Richard would have pancakes with lots of butter and maple syrup almost every morning. For snack, he might have a big glass of fruit juice and some cookies. For lunch, it was mac and cheese with french fries, and maybe candy for dessert. For dinner, Richard wanted more pasta, and bread with butter. He wouldn't eat vegetables, and the only fruit he ate was strawberries.

When he was four, Richard started to have trouble in preschool. He had a hard time staying in his seat or playing quietly with other kids. His teacher said he was "wild" most of the day, and sometimes he pushed or even hit other kids.

Richard's pediatrician thought he might have ADHD, and she explained that the first thing the family should do is get Richard on a healthier diet. "Cut out sugar," the pediatrician said, "even the fruit juice. Richard needs much more protein, whole grains, and vegetables in his diet."

Richard's mother knew that the doctor was right, but she couldn't imagine how to get Richard to eat food he didn't like. She just knew that every meal was going to be a big battle.

How is your diet? Do you think you need to change some of your eating habits?

_____

_____

_____

_____

For You to Do

Not too many people think you can change your diet all at once. It is usually best to change it a little at a time, eliminating a few unhealthy foods each week and substituting healthier foods at meals and snacks. Try doing this for one month, making just one change each week. Use the chart below to help you remember how important this is to your health. Each week, rate your success on a scale from 0 to 5, where 0 = no change and 5 = complete change.

	Food to Give Up	**Food to Eat in Its Place**	**Success Rating**
Week 1			
Week 2			
Week 3			
Week 4			

... And More to Do

Look at this list of foods. Grade each on how healthy you think they are for you:
1 = very good for you, 2 = has some value, or 3 = has very little value.

_____ Pizza

_____ Fried chicken

_____ White bread

_____ Scrambled eggs

_____ Broccoli

_____ Hamburger

_____ Sugarless gum

_____ Giant chocolate chip cookie

_____ Lowfat frozen yogurt

_____ Blueberries

For You to Know

Many kids with ADHD have difficulty sleeping. They may have a hard time falling asleep, or they may wake up during the night. When you don't get enough sleep, you will likely be irritable during the day, and you will have a harder time paying attention in school.

Logan hated to go to bed. His bedtime was nine o'clock, but he would find as many excuses as he could to stay up, and it was usually ten before his mother turned off the lights in his bedroom. He knew better than to turn the lights back on, but he hid a flashlight behind his bookshelf, and almost every night he would bring it under his blanket so he could read or play with his miniature cars.

Logan had better things to do than sleep. He'd much rather play or read. And he also had nightmares that bothered him sometimes. His worst nightmares were about skeletons that chased him around his backyard, trying to cut off his fingers and toes with their sharp sabers. Logan would rather not sleep at all than dream about those skeletons.

Every school morning, Logan's mother came in to wake him up at seven, and every day he would say, "Can't I just sleep a little longer?"

"No, you can't," his mother would say. "If you would go to sleep on time, you wouldn't be so tired in the morning. Now you'll just have to suffer the consequences and be tired all day."

And Logan did suffer the consequences of not sleeping, but he still kept trying to stay up as late as he could.

Do you go right to sleep, or do you fight to stay awake? How many hours do you sleep each night?

_____

_____

_____

_____

For You to Do

Most kids need nine to ten hours of sleep each night, so if you have to wake up at 6:00 a.m., you need to go to bed between 8:00 p.m. and 9:00 p.m. If you wake up at 7:00 a.m., you can go to bed between 9:00 p.m. and 10:00 p.m. If you are tired when you wake up and can't get out of bed, then you need to go to bed earlier.

Many kids say they can't fall asleep at night. If this is true for you, here are some things you need to do:

- Don't argue with your parents about your bedtime. Getting enough sleep is important for good health.

- Start relaxing an hour before bedtime. Do quiet activities, like reading or listening to peaceful music, rather than activities that wind you up, like playing a video game or a competitive board game.

- Try not to eat for at least two hours before bedtime. Certainly avoid foods with sugar or caffeine in them.

- Try not to sleep with a light on. The light will confuse your brain into thinking it is still daytime.

- Keep to a bedtime ritual. Try to do the same thing each night before you go to bed.

Write your bedtime ritual in the space below.

_____

_____

_____

_____

_____

... And More to Do

If you have a hard time relaxing, you could try imagining yourself in a quiet, peaceful place. Here are some ideas of places to imagine. Pick the scene that you like best, and draw it in the space below. Put in as much detail as you can, and look at this picture just before you go to bed.

- Imagine that you are floating on a cloud.

- Imagine that you are taking a quiet walk in the woods.

- Imagine that you are sitting on a beach, listening to the waves.

- Imagine that you are sailing on a boat across a calm, clear sea.

Helping Children Gain Self-Confidence, Social Skills, and Self-Control

Activity 38

You Can Limit Your TV and Video Game Time

For You to Know

Almost all kids like to play electronic games and watch TV. It's fine to do these activities some of the time, but not too much of the time. Spending too much time in front a TV or computer screen can be very unhealthy for you.

Ian was fantastic at almost any video game. Whether he was driving a car, fighting dragons, or playing virtual football, Ian always scored higher than his friends. Of course, Ian had plenty of practice. He spent hours every day playing video games on the computer, on his handheld game machine, and on the TV.

Ian's parents thought that he was spending too much time playing video games, but when they tried to get him to do other activities, he complained so much that they usually gave up. His father said to his mother, "I guess there are worse things than playing video games. At least he's learning coordination and to think fast. Maybe Ian will be a game designer when he grows up."

Ian's mother didn't say anything back. All she could think about was what Ian was missing— walking through the woods, riding around on his bike, drawing or painting, and so much more. She wished she could get Ian interested in other things besides playing electronic games, but she didn't know where to begin.

How many hours do you play video games or watch TV each day? Do you think this is too much time?

_____

_____

_____

_____

For You to Do

You have probably heard that spending too much time in front of a TV or computer screen can be a problem, but it is worth thinking about this some more. Check the statements that are true.

Kids who spend too much time in front of a screen

_____ tend to be more irritable.

_____ tend to put on weight.

_____ tend to get angrier easier.

_____ are not as physically fit as they could be.

_____ see more violence than they should.

_____ see a lot more commercials than other kids.

Which of these statements did you check? You should have checked all of them, because they are all true. Watching too much TV or spending too much time playing video games would be like eating candy for breakfast, lunch, and dinner. And that wouldn't be healthy, would it?

You Can Limit Your TV and Video Game Time

... And More to Do

Can you go on a TV and video game diet? Use the chart below to see just how many hours of TV you watch or video games you play in a week. Fill in the number of hours at the end of the day. You might be surprised at the results.

	Mon	Tues	Wed	Thurs	Fri	Sat	Sun
Hours watching TV							
Hours playing computer games							
Total hours							

If you spend more than fifteen hours a week in front of a screen, then you need to cut back. Write down ten things you can do besides watching TV or playing video games.

1. _____

2. _____

3. _____

4. _____

5. _____

6. _____

7. _____

8. _____

9. _____

10. _____

Activity 39

You Can Be a Responsible Kid

For You to Know

Learning responsibility is an important part of growing up. Kids have to learn to be responsible for their things. They have to remember their assignments and keep their schoolwork organized and neat. But that is just the beginning. Kids also have to be responsible for their pets, for the environment, for helping out at home, and more. It's a big job, but the more responsible you become, the better you will feel about yourself.

Shara came home from school at 4:00, and her mother didn't get home until 6:30. Shara had lots of things she was supposed to do every afternoon, including looking after her younger brother Bobby.

"Why didn't you clean up the living room?" Shara's mother asked. "There are toys and books all over the place."

"I had homework to do," Shara replied. "Isn't homework more important?"

"Well, did you get your homework done?" Shara's mother asked.

"Almost," Shara said, "but it was hard, and then Susannah called and I had to talk to her about something."

"And dinner?" Shara's mother said. "Did you start dinner like I asked?"

"Uh-oh," Shara said with a guilty smile. "I kind of forgot to turn on the oven like you said. But that was because Bobby had the TV so loud that my head was hurting and I forgot about dinner."

Shara's mother was exasperated. She said, "Do you have any more excuses for not doing what you were supposed to do?"

"I can't think of any," Shara said, but then she thought maybe that was not a good answer to give her mother.

How do you think her mother felt about Shara's behavior? What do you think Shara should do?

_____

_____

_____

_____

For You to Do

Are you responsible? The only way to measure responsibility is by your behavior. This test has fourteen responsible behaviors that kids should do. For one week, check off how many you do each day. See how many checks you can get.

Responsible Behavior	M	Tu	W	Th	F	Sa	Su	Total Checks
I did my chores without being asked.								
I did my homework without being asked.								
I kept my room neat and clean.								
I recycled.								
I turned off and/or unplugged my electronics.								
I took care of my clothes.								
I ate nutritious meals.								
I took care of my pets.								
I followed all the rules at school.								
I always told the truth.								
I played games by the rules.								
I was respectful to grown-ups.								
I was on time for school.								
I helped clean up after meals.								

... And More to Do

Think of people you know who are always responsible. Write down their names below. Ask them, "How do you remember to always do the right thing?" Write down their answers.

_____

_____

_____

_____

_____

_____

_____

_____

_____

_____

_____

> ## *For You to Know*
>
> Having ADHD usually means that you have different behavioral problems. You may have problems following rules at home and at school and you may often get into trouble. But everyone appreciates kids who are kind and helpful. When you are kind and helpful, adults will usually give you lots of positive attention and be more patient with your problems.

Almost everyone said that Lily was one of the nicest girls around. She always went out of her way to help someone out. She set the table at home without being asked. She picked up trash from her classroom and the school playground. If she saw a friend looking sad, she always asked what was wrong and offered to help if she could.

But Megan was jealous of Lily because she had so many friends and, in particular, because Lily was best friends with Kate. Megan said to Kate, "Don't you think that Lily is just a goody-goody? She always tries to be so perfect, but I bet she isn't perfect at all. I bet she does things that aren't nice and talks about people behind their backs."

"Do you mean like you're doing now?" Kate asked Megan. And Megan didn't have an answer for her.

"I like Lily just the way she is," Kate continued." She is nice to everyone, and that's the way people are supposed to be. There is nothing wrong with being nice."

"I guess," said Megan, not knowing what else to say.

"I wish more people were like Lily," Kate said.

"Yeah," said Megan, but she didn't sound like she really meant it.

Do you know someone who always tries to be kind and helpful, like Lily? Who are you most like in this story: Lily, Kate, or Megan?

_____

_____

_____

_____

For You to Do

Become a "kindness detective." Every day, look for ways to be kind and helpful, like Lily. Below are four boxes showing a classroom, a store, a playground, and a restaurant. Using stick figures, draw a picture of yourself doing something kind or helpful in each place.

... And More to Do

If you want to become a really kind and helpful person, you might want to take a notebook and make a "kindness diary." Each day, write down some kind or helpful thing you did for someone else. You can also write down nice things that other people do
for you.

Activity 41

You Can Have a More Peaceful Family

For You to Know

Every family has problems getting along with each other, but almost all of these problems can be solved. Having regular family meetings gives family members a chance to say what is on their minds and to suggest new solutions.

It seemed to Jeff that there was a lot of yelling in his home. Jeff's mom would yell at him for being too noisy and for tracking mud in the house. She would yell at Jeff's brother for talking back. His parents would sometimes yell at each other, too. His mom would say to his dad, "Why are you always late for everything? Can't you be on time for once?" And his dad would answer, "What's the big deal if I'm a few minutes late sometimes?"

There was so much yelling in Jeff's home that his parents decided they should all go to a family counselor. The counselor said, "I can see that you all love each other, but you have to learn to communicate in better ways. Yelling is stressful for all of you, and it can keep you from feeling happy." The counselor told Jeff's family to try having family meetings with clear rules. These are the rules he suggested:

- *A parent heads the family meeting. It should last no more than a half hour.*

- *Each person writes down something to talk about and presents it to the family.*

- *Everyone can say something about a problem, but there is no yelling, blaming, or interrupting.*

- *Always end a discussion about a problem with two possible solutions.*

- *Family meetings aren't just about problems. They should also include plans for activities and how to spend family fun time.*

- *End each meeting by having family members say one thing they appreciate about everyone in the group.*

Jeff's family had family meetings every Friday, and guess what happened?

Has your family ever had meetings? What happened?

_____

_____

_____

_____

For You to Do

If you have frequent arguments and disagreements in your home, you can suggest that your family have family meetings. Family meetings usually work best when they are held on a regular basis, like every week or every other week.

Write down five problems you would want to discuss at a family meeting.

1. _____

2. _____

3. _____

4. _____

5. _____

Write down five things other than problems you would want to discuss at a family meeting.

1. _____

2. _____

3. _____

4. _____

5. _____

... And More to Do

Show this activity to one or both of your parents and ask if you can have regular family meetings. Even if your family does not have arguments and everyone is happy, family meetings will help you communicate in positive ways, bringing the whole family closer together. Family meetings usually go best when they are organized. You can make copies of the page below to use at your family meeting. Your parents should fill in the page before the meeting begins.

What time will the meeting start and end? Start: _____ End: _____

Who will run the family meeting? _____

Things we will talk about:

1. _____

2. _____

3. _____

4. _____

Three important rules for the meeting:

1. _____

2. _____

3. _____

A fun way to end the meeting: _____

Things we decided at the meeting:

_____

_____

Activity 42   You Can Handle Being on Medication

> ## *For You to Know*
>
> Many kids with ADHD are on medication, and most say it helps them a great deal. But some kids have reactions to their medication, such as trouble sleeping, loss of appetite, or even stomachaches and headaches. Some kids don't have reactions like these, but they are still concerned about taking medication. They may worry that other kids will think that they are different, or they may worry about how the medication affects their brain. If your medication makes you feel strange in any way or causes you to worry, always tell your parents how you feel.

Nate's pediatrician wanted him to try a new type of medication for his ADHD. "You can take this medication once a day instead of three times a day," his pediatrician told him.

That sounded good to Nate. He particularly didn't like going to the school nurse every day. Even though none of the kids seem to care, Nate still didn't like the idea that some kids might think of him as being different.

But within a few days of taking the new medication, Nate started to get stomachaches. At first, Nate's mother thought he had a virus, but then she remembered that stomachaches were one of the side effects the doctor had mentioned.

Nate went back to his old medication. He was disappointed that he had to see the school nurse during the day again and asked his mother if he could just stop taking medication altogether.

"I know it can be hard," his mother said, "but your medication has really helped you. Your grades are better, you get along better with your sister, and you just seem happier when you are on it. Isn't that so?"

"I guess so," Nate said, "but I hope I won't have to take it forever."

"So do I," his mother said, giving Nate a hug, "so do I."

Have you ever had an experience with medication like Nate did? Who could you talk to if you have concerns about medication for your ADHD?

_____

_____

_____

_____

For You to Do

Nobody knows how you feel unless you tell them. This chart lists some side effects of taking medication for ADHD, and there is room for you to add others you may have had. Rate each statement on a scale from 1 to 3, where 1 = never, 2 = sometimes, and 3 = always. Show this chart to your parents when you are done.

Problem	Rating
I have stomachaches or feel nauseous.	
I feel nervous and jittery.	
I can't fall asleep at night.	
My mouth is dry.	
I have trouble making a bowel movement (constipation) or my bowel movements are loose (diarrhea).	
I get headaches or feel dizzy.	
I get rashes.	
I feel like my heart is racing.	
Other:	
Other:	

... And More to Do

Do you ever worry about taking medication for your ADHD? On the lines below, write down anything you worry about. Your parents want to know what you are thinking and feeling, so show them what you have written when you can.

_____

_____

_____

_____

_____

Activity 43   You Can Get Help When You Need It

For You to Know

It's great to be a kid, but sometimes it is hard, too. You might have problems with your friends, your schoolwork, your family, or even your health. But no matter what kind of problems you have, it helps to talk about things that bother you. Most kids talk to their parents when they have problems, but some kids prefer to talk to a counselor, a teacher, an aunt or uncle, or a grandparent.

Raphael was pretty happy. He liked his friends and his home, and he particularly liked playing soccer. But one morning, his dad said that he needed to talk to the whole family. They all sat down at the kitchen table.

"They are laying off people at my company," Raphael's father began, "and I'm one of them. It might be a while until I find another job."

Raphael didn't exactly know what would happen next. "Are we going to be poor?" he asked.

His dad smiled a little, and said, "No, but we'll have to make some changes, at least until I find a new job and maybe even after. We have to cut down on spending, and that means no family trips. We have to stop buying things that we don't really need." He took a deep breath and continued, "We might also have to move. If I can't find a job nearby, then we may have to move to another part of the country where there are more jobs for people with my experience."

"Move!" Raphael said. "But I love it here. What about my friends? What about my soccer team? They need me!" Raphael started to get very excited and worried. He really didn't want to move.

"Calm down," his father said. "I said that moving was only a possibility. I just wanted you to know everything that could happen so that you could be prepared."

"But I don't want to be prepared," Raphael told his dad, "because I don't want to move." And a few tears started to trickle down his cheek.

Have you ever had a big family problem that upset you? Who do you talk to when you have a big problem?

_____

_____

_____

_____

For You to Do

When you have a problem that you can't solve yourself, the best thing to do is to talk to someone and ask for help. Asking for help doesn't mean you will get exactly what you want. Sometimes the person you are talking to will offer an idea that is hard for you to do or that you don't like at all. That's okay. You can think about the advice you were given and try to use at least some of it. Or you can go to someone else for help.

Here are some kids who could use help. Write down the advice you would give each.

Teri's mom is very sick and in the hospital. Teri is worried that her mom won't get better and may even die. What advice would you give Teri?

_____

_____

_____

Bradley's bike was stolen. His dad had told him to lock up the bike, but he forgot and left it in the front yard. What advice would you give Bradley?

_____

_____

_____

Victoria had a hard time seeing the blackboard. She didn't want to wear glasses, so she didn't tell anyone. She would squint to see what her teacher had written on the board, but that didn't always work. What advice would you give Victoria?

_____

_____

_____

... And More to Do

Write down four people you can go to for help. Next to each name, write down the reasons you would want to get this person's advice.

1. _____   _____

                                        _____

2. _____   _____

                                         _____

3. _____   _____

                                         _____

4. _____   _____

                                         _____

For You to Know

If you have completed every activity in this workbook (or even most of them), you have learned a lot about ADHD. Congratulations! Learning about yourself is not like learning to read or learning science facts. It doesn't come just from books; it comes from talking to other people and it comes from life experience. Kids with ADHD often learn a lot from talking to other kids with ADHD. If you talk to other kids with ADHD, or even teens and grown-ups with ADHD, you can learn a lot about yourself.

Bea, Steve, Kyle, Lena, and Sam were all in a special club run by the school counselor, Mr. Reed. The club was called Power Kids. Its mission was to learn about ADHD. Each week, Mr. Reed would have a new topic for the members to talk about. One week they talked about ways to make friends. Another week they talked about homework. Another week they talked about famous people with ADHD.

The kids in the club were supposed to learn about their personal power. Mr. Reed said, "Having ADHD is just part of who you are. You could be tall or short or have glasses or freckles. You could be good at math or science or Ping-Pong or video games. The things you are good at are called your assets, and they are what makes you special. When you put all your assets together, you get your personal power."

Every week the Power Kids became a little more confident. Bea had been picked on before she joined the club, but no one seemed to tease her now. Sam had a reading problem, and although the problem didn't go away, he knew he could learn to read better with the help of his teacher, his parents, and his tutor. Kyle's teacher used to call him a "wild child," but not anymore. His teacher said to Kyle, "You've learned to calm down and pay attention, but you've also learned that you are a great kid. I'm very proud of you."

Do you know other kids with ADHD? Who could you ask to help you start a Power Kids Club?

_____

_____

_____

_____

For You to Do

To be a Power Kid, you just have to know your personal powers. Write down ten great things about yourself.

1. _____

2. _____

3. _____

4. _____

5. _____

6. _____

7. _____

8. _____

9. _____

10. _____

... And More to Do

Put your name and the date you finished this workbook on the following Certificate of Achievement. Write in three of your best qualities. You can also paste in a picture of yourself doing something you really like. When you are done, ask a parent or other adult to be your witness.

Certificate of Achievement

I, _____, (*your name*)
have learned a lot about my ADHD. I now know my personal
powers. They are

1. _____

2. _____

3. _____

Attach your
photo here.

Signed by

_____ on _____
(*your signature*)   (*date*)

Witnessed by

_____
(*a parent or adult*)

Lawrence E. Shapiro, Ph.D., is an internationally known child psychologist and parenting expert in Norwalk, CT. He has written over fifty books for parents, children, and mental health professionals.

more instant help books

Sign up for our **Book Alerts** at www.newharbinger.com

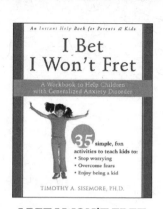

MY FEELING BETTER WORKBOOK

Help for Kids Who Are Sad & Depressed

US $16.95 / ISBN: 978-1572246126

LEARNING TO LISTEN, LEARNING TO CARE

A Workbook to Help Kids Learn Self-Control & Empathy

US $16.95 / ISBN: 978-1572245983

I BET I WON'T FRET

A Workbook to Help Children with Generalized Anxiety Disorder

US $16.95 / ISBN: 978-1572246003

Also available as an **eBook** at newharbinger.com

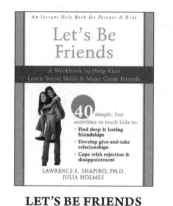

I'M NOT BAD, I'M JUST MAD

A Workbook to Help Kids Control Their Anger

US $16.95 / ISBN: 978-1572246065

LET'S BE FRIENDS

A Workbook to Help Kids Learn Social Skills & Make Great Friends

US $16.95 / ISBN: 978-1572246102

COPING WITH TOURETTE SYNDROME

A Workbook for Kids with Tic Disorders

US $16.95 / ISBN: 978-1572246324

Instant Help Books
A Division of New Harbinger Publications, Inc.

available from

new**harbinger**publications, inc.

and fine booksellers everywhere

To order, call toll free **1-800-748-6273** or visit our online bookstore at **www.newharbinger.com**

(VISA, MC, AMEX / prices subject to change without notice)

Check out www.psychsolve.com

PsychSolve™ offers help with diagnosis, including treatment information on mental health issues, such as depression, bipolar disorder, anxiety, phobias, stress and trauma, relationship problems, eating disorders, chronic pain, and many other disorders.